US-Soviet Relations During the Détente

Anne de Tinguy

EAST EUROPEAN MONOGRAPHS, BOULDER
DISTRIBUTED BY COLUMBIA UNIVERSITY PRESS, NEW YORK
1999

EAST EUROPEAN MONOGRAPHS, NO. DXXVI

Translated by A.P.M. Bradley

The translation from the French was made possible with the
financial assistance from the French Ministry of Culture

CONTENTS

INTRODUCTION   1

1. AN UNEASY COEXISTENCE, 1917-1970   3

2. THE LAUNCHING OF A NEW TYPE
    OF RELATIONS: THE DÉTENTE   15

3. ARMS CONTROL   31

4. TRADE BENEFITS   49

5. EXCHANGE OF
    TECHNOLOGY, IDEAS AND MEN   63

6. WHAT DID THE SUPERPOWERS WANT?   77

7. THE AMERICAN POINT OF VIEW:
    FROM CONFRONTATION TO NEGOTIATION   83

8. DIALOGUE FROM MOSCOW'S VIEWPOINT   105

9. DISAPPOINTMENTS   123

10. WHAT WAS LEFT OF DÉTENTE?   149

SELECTIVE BIBLIOGRAPHY   161

INTRODUCTION

We are not asking you to give up your principles or your friends, but you should not allow Hanoi through its intransigence to ruin the improved relations that together we have patiently established of late. We are at the start of a new era which could benefit the interests of our two countries, and also the cause of world peace. We are prepared to continue our progress in this direction. It is up to you whether we succeed or not.

These were the words uttered by Richard Nixon on May 8, 1972, after the American President, as a consequence of the latest North Vietnamese offensive, had announced his decision to intensify bombing and mine harbors in an effort to cut off Hanoi from its sources of supply—in other words, the Soviet Union. Considering the links binding the two countries, this was a bold decision taken only a few days before his planned visit to Moscow. Yet such a move was necessary if the United States was to cut a good figure in Moscow and retain any hope of reaching an "honorable" peace in Vietnam. The choice of words used in addressing the Soviet leaders meant a challenge was issued by Nixon. If the summit meeting did take place, the USSR publicly acknowledged that a dialogue with the top capitalist power was more important than supporting its North Vietnamese communist ally. If it were to be canceled, they would lose a chance of counter-balancing the US-China summit meeting of February 1972, forfeit the advantages of the agreements due to be signed in the course of the visit; further, the American change of mood might ruin the prospect of the West German parliament ratifying draft treaties with East Germany. The Soviet leaders were aware of the stakes and two weeks later, three months after his Peking visit, Nixon was received in the USSR with much pomp—this was the first time an American President made an official tour of the country. He did not leave empty-handed: the two superpowers reached a clear definition of the "fundamental principles" of their relations and an agreement, for the first time ever, on the steps to be taken to effect armament limitations.

The way this crisis was resolved indicated the main lines of the policy initiated by the USSR and the United States at the time, casting an unprecedented ray of hope on world relations, which would be known as détente. The two powers, after fifty years of profound hostility, were ready to listen to each other. They had no intention of

1

laying down arms, nor of forgetting about old rivalries, but meant to find ways of cooperating. Though they might have contrary ambitions, they wished to base their dealings on talk and negotiation. The Americans hoped that cooperation would gradually take precedence over opposition and that the Soviet conduct would become more restrained in the process, at least on the international scene. In the short term, if they succeeded in establishing a dialogue with the USSR, it would help them to bring an end to the Vietnam war and through a spectacular victory, regain the vitality lost in the Far Eastern quagmire. The Soviets had even more reasons to seek a rapprochement: it was the only way they had to counter the Chinese threat and avoid being isolated internationally; it was also an attractive way of compensating for the all too visible weaknesses of their political system. Détente came after prolonged and painstaking attempts at putting their relations with the United States on a normal footing. It constituted the corner-stone of their foreign policy, and represented a striking political victory: the United States acknowledged them as an international partner, a position such as they had never occupied in the past, or only during World War II, due to exceptional circumstances.

The Moscow summit was a decisive step in the development of this new relationship as well as highly symbolic. Yet the trip was only one gesture among many intended to establish better contacts. A new atmosphere of give and take and comradeship prevailed and the superpowers found themselves in a totally different situation in dealing with each other.

Yet in spite of sustained efforts, the initial results proved disappointing. Even though they were determined to seek a common ground, the superpowers soon found limitations to this enterprise: concrete achievements did not match expectations and, half way through the decade, a climate of confrontation had returned. Détente, however, though proving something of an empty word in later years, did bring real political, economic and strategic gains which, in different circumstances, might have imparted a new stability to relations between the two countries and the international situation. It is useful to examine the vital period of the early 70s when something emerged promising a better world order, if only to understand the reasons why it ended in failure and discover the conditions necessary for a more satisfactory outcome.

1

AN UNEASY COEXISTENCE, 1917-1970

The USSR and the United States have a long history of mutual distrust. To appreciate the novelty of the fruitful dialogue that went on in the 1970's and the hopes it aroused, one should remember how deep the rift between the two countries ran, how the path of their relations was strewn with disillusions, and realize that every attempt at better understanding had thus far failed miserably. The two world powers were not only kept apart by short-term differences, such as problems of borders, or even by the rivalry engendered by power. The conflict between them, apparently linked to contrasting ideologies and world views, was in fact embedded in their respective history. It loomed much larger the day the two countries were in possession of the atom bomb and were capable of destroying each other, together with a large part of our civilization.

A NEW KIND OF INTERNATIONAL RELATIONS

Since 1917, the USSR occupied a place apart in world politics. Advocating a new international order, asserting herself as totally different from the other states, Soviet Russia in the beginning refused to be a member of the community. Being the model for world revolution, it would have nothing to do with traditional international relations. In the early days, the Bolsheviks did not have in mind the creation of a Soviet state with its own boundaries and acknowledged rights. They considered themselves as a revolutionary proletarian power, whose mission was to change the nature of society everywhere so as to reflect the popular will, and as such did not recognize national frontiers. They were convinced of the imminence of world revolution, especially in Europe, and saw it as a requirement for their own survival. Their first gesture in foreign policy, the peace decree of October 26, 1917, was an appeal to the will of peoples above the head of governments, a revolutionary appeal which indicated their intention of dealing with international problems from the point of view of the world revolution. Trotsky, the head of the People's Commissariat of Foreign Affairs, was quite sure that, after making the secret agreements public, his department would lose its *raison d'être*.

3

This revolutionary dream could not resist the onslaught of reality for long: the peace decree evoked no popular response; the European laboring masses did not rise to help their "Russian revolutionary brothers." The Bolsheviks were then forced to think of their national interest and turn to existing governments to open negotiations, that is, the Central Powers. The peace treaty was signed on March 3, 1918, at Brest-Litovsk. All revolutionary illusions were completely shattered between 1918 and 1921: in Hungary in 1919 (when Bela Kun failed to retain power) and in Germany during the same year with the collapse of the Spartakist movement and demise of the short-lived Soviet Republic in Munich. In 1919 there was the abortive March coup; in 1920 factories were occupied for a short time in Italy; in Poland the same thing happened that year. The outcome of the Baku Conference (September, 1920) was also disappointing. These reversals made coexistence with the capitalist system inevitable and the world revolution came to coincide with the socialist motherland: Soviet power had to be protected. Internal development followed the same path. In 1920-21, Lenin had to admit that the country needed a breathing space: the start of negotiations with other countries (primarily on the borders), was meant to stabilize relations with the outside world at the time when the NEP was launched (February, 1921).

The years 1917-1921 were crucial for the establishment of the guidelines of Soviet foreign policy. The fact that it was impossible for the Bolsheviks to set up a new international order did not mean that they would renounce their revolutionary principles; rather, it led to a system combining these principles and the reality confronting them on which their relations with the outside world would rest. The aim of a world revolution was not abandoned, it merely became more distant in time. The change affected tactics, but the objective remained the same. Until the "spark" came, the Soviet Union must enter the international scene, build up its internal and external power, guarantee at all costs the state's security—in short, live with other countries and negotiate with the capitalist powers in the traditional manner.

The policy of peaceful coexistence goes back to those days, when Lenin decided that the USSR had to negotiate deals with a social and political system contrary to its own. The socialist motherland prided itself on being the center of the world revolutionary movement; it acted both as a state among others and one with a mission. Being pragmatic, it had no qualms about abandoning its principles for a while, if the situation demanded it.

LENIN AND THE UNITED STATES

Early on, the Bolsheviks felt the need to differentiate between the various capitalist countries and not to show the same animosity towards them. Their attitude to the United States is a good illustration of this.

Unlike some European countries, especially Germany or Poland, the United States was not considered to be, in the short term, a favorable ground for revolution. The Bolsheviks repeatedly appealed to the American "laboring masses," but these appeals, above all after American troops had landed on Soviet territory, were a defense mechanism more than anything else. The Bolsheviks had once believed the United States to be more favorably disposed towards them than the other western countries. Yet the notion of American "friendship" did not survive the intervention.

In spite of this set-back, the United States remained high on the list of Soviet priorities for two reasons. One had to do with the international balance of power: if the United States was opposed to Germany and, even more to the point, Japan, the threat posed by the West would be lessened. Encouraging conflicts among capitalist countries was the best guarantee of security for the Soviet power in its early years. The other reason concerned the American impressive economic power which showed great promise for commercial exchanges: the United States having been spared by the war would become their first client, as Germany used to be before 1914.

Consequently, Lenin established surprisingly good relations with the United States, a country for which he felt a strong attraction. His first attempts proved unsuccessful: President Wilson did not respond to the incredible offer of increased economic links made in May, 1918; instead he refused to let any representative of the Soviet regime enter the country and decided to have American troops participate in anti-Bolshevik operations on Soviet territory. Yet the United States was the first to send substantial humanitarian aid in the summer of 1921 when Russia and the Ukraine were struck by a catastrophic famine. On July 5, Maxim Gorki appealed for outside help and almost immediately the ARA (American Relief Administration), under the direction of H. Hoover, came to the rescue. Foodstuffs and medicines were sent to Russia in the following months, to the tune of about $85 million, saving the lives of some 10 million people.

Hoover was not the only one to hear the Bolshevik appeal. A young American, A. Hammer, who happened to be on Soviet soil in the summer of that year, appalled by the living conditions of the population of the Urals, organized supplies of cereals on a large scale with credit facilities for the Russians. Lenin asked to meet him to show his gratitude; this was the beginning of a fruitful friendship between them. Hammer took out concessions on Soviet territory, remained in the country until 1931 and returned on several occasions to sign important contracts. A few months earlier, Lenin was greatly tempted by the generous offers made to him by another American, B. Vanderlip, whom he mistook for his namesake, a well-known banker, a close friend of president-to-be Harding. He thought it was politically wise to establish individual relations with Americans to breach the feeling of hostility prevalent in the country towards the new regime in Russia.

Being realistic, Lenin saw nothing wrong in opening his borders to American aid, nor in establishing commercial relations with a country whose government rejected him through contacts with personalities willing to talk to him. He wrote in September, 1917, "The duty of a truly revolutionary party does not lie in refusing all compromises, but in spite of compromises, insofar as they are inevitable, to remain faithful to one's principles, class, revolutionary objective and prepare for the revolution...." On October 5, 1919, he declared "We are fully in favor of an economic agreement with America, with all countries, but with America above all." There is no doubt that he saw no incompatibility between the revolutionary vocation of Soviet Russia and friendly relations with the top capitalist power. Before another wave of revolutions could start, the Soviet state had to be strengthened: he encouraged cooperation with the United States as a powerful factor to this end. The politics of peaceful coexistence had no other meaning to Lenin's mind.

Throughout the 1920's and the early 1930's, the American government continued its policy of cold-shouldering the new regime. This attitude was based on three reasons: the Soviet regime was not representative; it did not respect the international commitments of its predecessor; its objective of world revolution could not be reconciled with normal inter-state relations. In short, the US was convinced that they had nothing in common "with a power whose conception of international relations was so contrary to their own and completely opposed to moral sense." Secretary of State Colby wrote in 1920 that the American government felt "repelled" by the Soviet state. Under the circumstances, he thought that "recognizing it and entering negotiations with it would mean sacrificing morality for the sake of material advantages which will prove short-lived and costly." Yet throughout these early years of industrial production in Soviet Russia, the Americans were involved together with Europeans and Japanese in bringing vital technical help, albeit on a modest scale. In 1930-31, Ford built a huge car plant at Gorki, similar to the one at River Rouge in the United States. General Electric built a giant factory for manufacturing turbines in 1930-33. The United States humiliated the USSR and rejected it, while considerably contributing to the growth of the regime, though it is difficult to estimate by how much. Coexistence, in spite of non-recognition, proved to be greatly beneficial to the USSR.

BELATED RECOGNITION

It was not until November, 1933, sixteen years after the Bolshevik revolution that the United States recognized the USSR. Obstacles to the establishment of diplomatic relations, as defined immediately after the revolution, remained. On the other hand, circumstances had changed and the USSR had proved the stability of its regime. It was imperative to be on good terms to preserve peace in the extremely tense international situation created by Hitler's rise to power and Japanese aggressiveness. In the context of a serious economic crisis there might be advantages in renewed contacts. Franklin D. Roosevelt, who became President of the United States on March 4, 1933, fully conscious of pressing problems thought it would be possible to solve them through a global approach. After recognizing the USSR, the American government concluded several agreements with her. One dealt with the payment of debts incurred by previous Russian governments. Another concerned the Soviet government's commitment not to intervene in any way in American internal affairs, to refrain from propaganda campaigns or agitation which might disturb public order, security, territorial integrity, or the social and political organization of the country. A third one concerned the respect of religious freedom and freedom of opinion of the American citizens who were resident in the USSR. This attempt at an overall approach ended in failure. The vague wording of the agreements—in respect of non-interference, the Comintern, the arm of world revolution, was not even mentioned; regarding the debt, there was no mention of the exact figure—reflected the impossibility of settling differences. The Soviet government went on claiming that there was no connection between the Comintern and the Soviet state, the latter therefore could not be held responsible for the actions of the former. It refused to allow any validity to the protest made by the American government at the time of the 7th Congress of the Comintern in Moscow in July-August, 1935, when the question of communist propaganda in the United States was raised. As to the talks on clearing the debt, they ended in February, 1935, in an impasse.

Thus recognition, which proved a great political victory for the USSR, did not help solve other problems: feelings of suspicion replaced downright hostility and a climate of misunderstanding reigned.

During the war, things seemed more promising. The Americans sensed a different attitude in the USSR and hoped that after the end of the conflict a new era would open.

THE GREAT ALLIANCE

The primary objective of the Great Alliance was to defeat Hitler. Yet Roosevelt saw in it more than military cooperation; it was part of a vast plan for reorganizing the international balance of power after the war. In the event of victory over Nazism, he thought that the United States, the USSR and Great Britain would emerge from the conflict in a strong position, and on condition that they remained united, the three countries could preserve peace and prevent the eruption of future conflicts, by force if necessary. Because this objective implied close relations, it made it imperative to dispel the atmosphere of distrust separating the USSR and the United States. If the two countries trusted each other, the United Nations Organization would ensure security for the Soviet Union; it would therefore put up with the capitalist environment and remain within the terms of the alliance.

The course taken by Soviet politics was encouraging, in Roosevelt's opinion as well as that of many Americans. The Comintern, being more discrete in the pre-war period, had not held a congress since 1935, and its dissolution on May 22, 1943, was interpreted as a sign that the conflict between the USSR and the western world was becoming less acute. Many Americans believed Soviet leaders to be less preoccupied by the idea of world revolution as they seemed increasingly concerned by strictly national problems. The nationalistic political line taken by Stalin during the war supported this thesis, while the courage shown by the Soviet armed forces and the respect of military commitments on the part of Stalin did much to improve the image of the Soviet Union in the United States. President Roosevelt had no illusions as to the totalitarian character of the Soviet political system; he was not trying to change it, but to transform the war alliance into "business relations" and make the USSR more tolerant through constant dealings between them.

This hope was somewhat clouded by difficulties arising over cooperation in the field, even in wartime. The policy of aid to the USSR—the Lease-Lend program—intended by Roosevelt to be generous, with no strings attached, was not sufficient to convince the USSR of the sincerity of American goodwill. It did not compensate for delays in opening a second front. The Soviet leaders did not believe the argument of material shortages could explain why it was postponed until June, 1944, and saw in the delay an attempt on the part of the Allies to impose the burden of the war effort on the USSR so as to leave the country weakened when hostilities ended. They thought the United States was giving them just enough aid to prevent a total collapse, which would have proved catastrophic for all concerned, but was not willing to go any further.

The policy applied by the Soviets in Eastern Europe was quick to recall the specter of world revolution to the Americans' minds. Each crisis in this area raised doubts as to the merits of the alliance and the possibility of future cooperation. The explosion of an atomic bomb and its use against Japan in August, 1945, increased tension between the Allies. In the prevailing climate, it was inevitable that the Soviet leaders should be alarmed. The Great Alliance, far from proving the start of an era of cooperation, marked a breakdown in relations between the two countries.

SOVIET EXPANSION MUST BE CURBED

The international situation after the war was completely different from what it had been before 1939. The emerging bipolar world was characterized by headlong clashes. The American and Soviet governments soon reached the conclusion that the "other" entertained sinister designs, that their national objectives were antagonistic and their interests incompatible. Soviet foreign policy in the post-war period was one of expansion. Between 1945 and 1949, by means of political influence and sometimes the presence of the Red Army, the USSR spread its ideology and domination throughout Eastern Europe: in Poland, Hungary, Romania and Bulgaria the Communists took over power. Henceforth the Soviet Union found herself, on its western borders, protected from the capitalist world by a belt of People's Democracies; she lost no time in consolidating her hold in the region. In this context, the intrusion of Soviet troops in Iran in 1946 and the outbreak of civil war in Greece in 1947 seemed to signal the USSR's intention to expand and its hostility towards the "free world."

On March 12, 1947, President Truman called on the American Congress to "support free peoples resisting attempts to reduce them to slavery through armed minorities or external pressures" and asked for a grant of $400 million for Greece and Turkey to help them ensure their independence. This declaration, the basis of what is called the Truman Doctrine, meant that, from that time on, the security of the United States was at risk everywhere "a direct or indirect attack" threatened a country's freedom, and that behind every local crisis the United States saw the shadow of a Soviet "conductor" and that they were prepared to thwart any sign of expansion on the part of the USSR.

A few months later, in July, 1947, the head of a team in charge of political forecasting of the Department of State, George Kennan, calling himself X, published an article in *Foreign Affairs* in which he advocated the need to curb Soviet power. The Soviet state, according to him, in its policies followed ideological principles which bore on the future: inevitability of the collapse of capitalism and inherent antagonism between capitalist and socialist countries. This basic disagreement, from Moscow's point of view, made it impossible to establish any common standpoint between the USSR and the capitalist countries. To confront Soviet behavior, Kennan judged that "the main element of any American policy must consist in containing patiently, but firmly and with vigilance, the expansionist tendencies of Russia." Threats, occasional shows of activity, or a passive attitude could serve no purpose. The United States must adopt "a policy of firm limitations, intended to confront the Russians with an unshakable barrier wherever the latter show any intention of damaging the interests of a peaceful and stable world." This analysis, which corresponded to what everyone in Washington more or less clearly thought, was well-timed and met with general agreement. Containment of the USSR, from then on and for a long time to come, became the central rule of American policy.

The USSR had already withdrawn from the international scene; it was now fighting tooth and nail against cosmopolitan tendencies, re-appraising the wartime alliance and making declarations on the impossibility of reconciliation. In the United States friendship for an old ally was replaced by a fierce anti-communist campaign which, from 1947, assumed a disproportionate role in political life: the period of McCarthy's influence and witch-hunts had started.

The Soviet response to the Marshall Plan caused a rift between East and West. The Prague coup, putting the final touch to political changes in Eastern Europe, the Berlin blockade (June, 1948 – May, 1949), and later the Korean conflict reinforced the Western belief in Soviet hostility. The breach had become public, even before the Korean flare-up, with the signing by five European countries in Brussels, on March 17, 1948, of a treaty of mutual assistance, referring to "any attack." Then followed the signing of the Atlantic Pact in Washington, on April 4, 1949, the setting up of two Republics in Germany—one Federal, the other Democratic—in May and October, 1949. The two blocs became practically isolated from each other. The two Great Powers launched programs of re-armament (the Soviets, after the Americans, perfected the A-bomb in 1949 and the H-bomb in 1953), completely changing the terms of their struggle.

THE THAW

After Stalin's death, the gap between the two blocs widened with Germany joining NATO late in 1954 and the signing of the Warsaw Pact in May, 1955. Yet it did not take long before Western countries realized that the situation was changing. The Soviet leaders proved unexpectedly amenable on a number of points which had been responsible for increased East-West tension in previous years. In Korea, negotiations were resumed on April 27, 1953, and three months later an armistice was signed. On April 26, 1954, talks started in Geneva on the subject of Korea and more significantly on Indochina: Molotov not only refrained from raising obstacles, he put pressure on the Vietminh to reach an agreement; by July 20, an armistice was signed. In May, 1955, the four great powers signed a treaty which gave Austria back its freedom: all foreign soldiers were to clear Austrian soil in the following weeks. It was the first time since they had evacuated their troops from Iran that the Soviets had given up an occupied territory. While signing the treaty, the Big Four agreed to hold a summit conference which started on July 18 of the same year, in Geneva. The Soviets did not spare efforts to end the state of isolation they were in and which had become unbearable; indeed, they wished to re-enter the international community alongside the Western countries.

Other changes were on the way. The break with Stalinism which had quickly become apparent after the leader's death (leading to amnesties, reconciliation with Yugoslavia, etc.) was made public during the 20th Congress of the CPSU in February, 1956. On this occasion, Khrushchev shook his country's whole political outlook by denouncing Stalin's crimes and laying new foundations for foreign policy. He stressed the possibility and even the necessity of peaceful coexistence due to the nuclear factor and growing power of the USSR and the socialist camp. From acting as a besieged fortress doomed to remain defensive, the USSR had turned offensive. The capitalist world was now besieged, on the one hand by the socialist camp whose power was rising fast and on the other, by the Third World, which, as Khrushchev fully realized, was to play a vital part in the international balance of power. Stalin had considered the world as being split into two realms: capitalism and communism. Khrushchev divided it in three, attributing an intrinsic value to neutral countries inasmuch as they stood against imperialism. While proclaiming peaceful coexistence, he questioned the theory that wars were inevitable so long as imperialism existed; he preferred to believe that the most complex difficulties in international relations could be settled by negotiations. The statement he made on the many paths to socialism, in contradiction to Stalin who did not envisage anything apart from the Soviet model, was a confirmation that a revolution was taking place. This change of direction did not affect only the international posture of the USSR. The claim that the USSR was like a besieged fortress, that a permanent threat was hanging over it, had enabled Stalin to justify his authoritarian regime. Was a more tolerant one to follow? The answer was no. Peaceful coexistence did not mean ideological reconciliation: the USSR must remain wary of a weakening of the system in its wake. Coexistence meant peaceful competition in all areas, rivalry without war between two systems, the better of which—that is to say, to the communist leader's mind, communism—will emerge victorious. He seemed very self-assured and convinced of his country's superiority: the USSR, he added, would catch up with the United States and overtake them (an objective to be reached by 1970, he declared at the 22nd Congress of the CPSU in 1961). He was to repeat this slogan over and over again to justify all his economic demands. Competing, but also coming to an understanding with the United States were the main Soviet concerns at the time: in 1956 a treaty of "non-aggression, friendship and non-interference" was suggested, to be valid for twenty years, and in 1958, the normalization of commercial relations. As a result international relations did become less tense.

   These positive gestures, at a time when Dulles was at the helm of the State Department (1953-1959), were not likely to arouse much enthusiasm in the United States. They did not fit the picture of the USSR the Secretary of State had in mind. He was convinced of the Communists' ingrained antagonism to the "free world" and saw in Khrushchev's policy nothing but a stratagem in the savage struggle between the two enemy powers. The Americans were at the time deeply alarmed by the scientific advances of the Soviet Union which, as well as scoring undeniable economic successes, had developed the hydrogen bomb (only a few months later than themselves) and launched their first intercontinental ballistic missile (ICBM), followed by the first space rocket (the Sputnik). Such realizations gave a measure of the scientific capabilities of the Soviet Union along with their military implications. The late 1950's was a period when everyone was frightened of a "missile gap," of being overtaken by the USSR. This led to an acceleration of armament programs on the part of the United States. The likelihood of better relations was thus practically nil.

   Did Nikita Khrushchev believe that the USSR would overtake its adversary (as he boasted on his visit to the US in 1959) through a policy of coexistence? That may be so, but for lack of a positive response the Soviet leaders chose to improve their position by carry-ing out several coups. The early 1960's were a period of extreme tension. In May, 1960, after a Soviet rocket brought down an American U-2 reconnaissance airplane above Sverdlovsk, Eisen-hower refused to apologize. Khrushchev, in a rage, abruptly left the summit conference taking place four days later in Paris, with the four Big Powers present, and postponed Eisenhower's visit to the

USSR that was to occur in June. In April, 1961, John Kennedy organized a landing of anti-Castro forces in Cuba (the Bay of Pigs operation). Two months later, in Vienna, he found Khrushchev unwilling to reach any agreement on the question of Berlin. Relations were more strained than ever.

THE CUBAN CRISIS

On August 13, 1961, the Soviet leaders decided to build a wall in Berlin to split the city into two; the West protested, but had to accept the fait accompli. A few months later, in Cuba, the USSR struck again, so that the superpowers found themselves on the brink of war (October, 1962). By installing rockets on Cuban soil, was the USSR trying to tilt the strategic balance to its advantage and gain the upper hand just before the planned negotiations on Berlin? Did the leaders assume that the United States would bow to the new situation in this case also? If so, they soon stood corrected: the American reaction was quick and sharp. The crisis ended with the withdrawal of rockets by Moscow; on the strength of this, the Americans promised not to invade Cuba.

This crisis was to have a lasting effect on the two countries. The USSR had become aware of its limitations vis-à-vis the United States. In the following years a sustained effort was made to wipe out the humiliation it had suffered; the armament drive went into higher gear, especially in the strategic and naval fields. The superpowers had been so shocked by the confrontation that henceforth they tended to respect the status quo. They had both learnt a lesson and felt the need to apply new rules in dealing with their rival. The Soviet Union from then on refrained from directly threatening the West. In June, 1963, the leaders of the two countries, to avoid a misunderstanding in the event of a crisis, had a "red telephone line" installed. Two months later, in Moscow, they signed a treaty on the suspension of nuclear tests in the atmosphere, in space and under the sea, which in view of the Chinese opposition to it, showed clearly where the Soviets stood. In June, Kennedy called for a re-examination of their relations towards more tolerance.

The end of the 1960's was a period of re-armament for the Soviet Union, which after a few years enabled it to enter talks with the United States on an equal footing, and to seek ways of lessening the risks of an open conflict. The next decade would prove that détente had thus been made possible.

2

THE LAUNCHING OF A NEW TYPE
OF RELATIONS: THE DÉTENTE

The summit meetings of May, 1972, June, 1973 and November, 1974 provided a background for negotiations. Could the incredible happen? Could a 55 years-long struggle finally end in reconciliation? This eventuality looked more likely as meetings followed one another and exchanges became more commonplace. The leaders of both countries, seemingly eager to make up for lost time, set down to work in earnest. They demanded better relations in all directions and results soon followed. The possibility of dialogue was restored, with control of armaments taking pride of place, but commercial links, as well as scientific and technical cooperation, were encouraged. Communications became easier; a number of common enterprises were planned; contracts and agreements were signed daily, mixed commissions were established and a completely new infrastructure was set up. After a post-war period when contacts were non-existent and, in the 1960's, a few feeble efforts were made, suddenly the next decade saw a burst of activity. At last, 40 years after diplomatic relations had been reestablished, normal relations were becoming possible. This revolution was primarily due to political decisions; if it had not been the case, the serious problems dividing the two countries would have kept them apart.

DÉTENTE IN SPITE OF VIETNAM

When Richard Nixon flew to Moscow on May, 1972, to everyone's surprise, he had many reasons to celebrate: a transformation had occurred in East-West relations. In order to entertain the American President, the Soviet leaders had gone back on their commitment to their Vietnamese ally. They gave preference to the most powerful among capitalist countries at the expense of a Third World communist state which had, over many years, become a symbol of resistance in the face of imperialism. Nixon had his dream turn into reality: Hanoi was now isolated.

He had to work hard to achieve this. Vietnam had plagued him from the early days of his term in office: for seven years, the United States had been embroiled in a costly war with a small country they called Indochina, the latter receiving most of its armaments and considerable economic assistance from the USSR. During his electoral campaign of 1968, Nixon had promised to bring the conflict to an end. Yet, at the start of his fourth year as president, success was nowhere in sight. Military victory was no longer an objective—a dignified exit was now his only ambition. However, even this modest requirement seemed out of reach in the spring of 1972. In March-April, Hanoi launched a full-scale offensive on several fronts; in the north the de-militarized zone separating the two parts of Vietnam since 1954 was invaded. Hanoi soon had the advantage in the struggle and the South Vietnam regime came under threat. If Nixon was to avert a disaster (that is to say, avoid signing a peace treaty dictated by North Vietnam) and be able to go to Moscow without feeling humiliated, he had to take the situation in hand. His difficulty was that the means at his disposal were limited: he had only a small expeditionary force (reduced from 545,000 men when he was elected to only 69,000); public opinion in the United States was increasingly opposed to a continuation of the war; the outcome of the campaign of Vietnamization was uncertain and the Paris negotiations with North Vietnam had produced no results. On May 2 (Leonid Brezhnev had hinted a few days earlier about putting pressure on his allies), Henry Kissinger met Le Duc Tho, who again proved as inflexible than ever. Under the circumstances, Nixon resorted to a measure which was bound to please the American public, the sea blockade of North Vietnam. With no supplies going through, Hanoi would be forced to downgrade the offensive and might prove more conciliatory. The only problem remaining—a sizable one—was that this solution was a slap in the face for the USSR. What would be the Soviet reaction?

On May 8, after the blockade was announced, the members of Nixon's team fully expected the Kremlin to cancel the summit meeting. They were much relieved at the mild reaction that followed. On May 11, the Soviet government condemned the American decision and stated that "the USSR would draw the necessary conclusions." When these became known, it was clear that US fears had been exaggerated. Foreign Trade Minister N. Patolichev, who happened to be in Washington on May 8, did not cut his visit short but asked to meet Nixon. As for the Soviet Ambassador to Washington, Dobrynin, he did not link the Vietnam problem to the summit: preparations could go ahead. The trial of strength was over. Richard Nixon's bet of showing his mettle in Vietnam had succeeded: the summit would take place and Hanoi was isolated. The Americans had proved that their quest for détente did not take precedence over other vital interests. The triumph of a rapprochement with the USSR, and later with China, was of enormous importance and spurred Nixon on in looking for a solution to the difficulties generated by the war in Indochina.

Why did the USSR make it easy for the Americans? Why wasn't the summit meeting canceled? Not only did the decision suit the United States, it was bound to raise doubts among Third World countries (this was especially true of Egypt) and shake communist certainties as to their ideological position.

It was not an easy decision for the Soviet leaders to sacrifice their support of the Vietnamese communists in this spectacular fashion for the sake of détente with Washington. They stressed the point during the summit talks. On May 22, President Nixon was greeted in Moscow less than enthusiastically. At the airport a thin group of people was lined behind barriers waving paper banners. The drive to the Kremlin took place along deserted roads at high speed (Nixon was able to observe in adjacent streets large crowds kept well back from the cortege of official cars). The Soviet government made sure the American President remained isolated throughout the visit.

The first contact with Leonid Brezhnev, who had not waited for his visitor at the airport, was noticeably cool; the Secretary General made it clear that he had trouble going ahead with the summit meeting in view of recent developments in Vietnam. "Only the utmost importance given to improving American-Soviet relations and the possibility of an agreement on certain problems has allowed it." Such a remark was repeated as an introduction to any discussion, thus showing the American leaders that their moderation was appreciated. Yet the subject of Vietnam did not figure prominently in the talks. In reality, the Soviet leaders made it the center of discussions at one session only, but the occasion was rather special. On May 24, after a peaceful boat outing in the country, Brezhnev suggested they had a talk in his dacha before dinner: within a few seconds, all suggestion of good humor and conviviality had vanished to be replaced by insults and accusations. For three hours, the three leaders—Brezhnev, Kosygin and Podgorny—took Nixon to task on the matter of his Vietnam policy. Kosygin mentioned the possibility that the North Vietnamese might accept foreign troops fighting alongside their own. This was the last time the Americans heard such a threat. The confrontation ended without a discussion taking place; the atmosphere over dinner was relaxed. It felt like a game or an interlude, Henry Kissinger wrote in his *Memoirs* (pp. 1279-1285); when the Soviets "had spoken long enough to be able to send a report to Hanoi," they ceased their ranting. A few days later (June 15-18), Podgorny went to Vietnam to reassure the military that Soviet support would continue. Yet actions spoke louder than words: the USSR had given precedence to the USA. There was nothing to add, which was why the topic was given scant attention at the summit meeting. In the following months, intensive bombing by the Americans evoked no response from the Soviet Union.

Moscow undoubtedly decided to talk to Nixon in spite of his policy in Indochina because of the current US rapprochement with China. Though little was said about Vietnam during the first summit meeting, even less was said about China and yet the PRC was obviously of the greatest importance to the Soviets. It is most likely that, if Nixon had not made his trip to Peking in February, he would not have been received in Moscow three months later, in the middle of the Vietnam crisis. The question of China was only hinted at. During the "talk" on Vietnam, Brezhnev accused Nixon of trying "to use the Chinese in order to force the Soviets to intervene in Vietnam"; on the eve of the President's departure, he made it clear that it would be in the two countries' interest to closely watch Peking's nuclear progress.

Later on, the attitude of the Soviets left no doubt as to their state of mind concerning US rapprochement with China. The latter was the backdrop of all the debates which took place in the following months to reach an agreement on the prevention of nuclear war. What the Soviets initially suggested was a treaty banning the use of nuclear weapons, but the Americans were convinced that this was a ploy to ensure that the Unites States would not side with the Chinese in the event of a war between the USSR and China. In March, 1973, at Zavidovo, during a shooting outing with Henry Kissinger, Brezhnev suddenly burst into a violent attack on China and used threatening language. The USSR, he said, could not stand in the wings while China acquired nuclear capability; the growth of Chinese military power was dangerous for the USSR and the whole world, so much so that any military assistance to the PRC would lead to war. The next day, Dobrynin took the matter up again and stressed the importance of the Secretary-General's words. At San Clemente, where the second summit meeting took place, Brezhnev expressed his fears more forcefully: the Chinese, he said, were aggressive by nature and "within ten years, they will have caught up with us in the field of armaments." The USSR had no intention of attacking the PRC, but a US-China military agreement "would make the problem singularly more complicated." This time it was Andrei Gromyko who, a few hours later, facing Kissinger, made clear the implications of Brezhnev's words: any military agreement between China and the United States would lead to war.

In these exceptional circumstances, the first decisive step towards détente was thus taken, following several months of timid preparation. The need to ward off the danger of rapprochement between China and the United States lay behind the Soviet leaders' determination to establish privileged relations with Washington. The American leaders had other worries, but the stakes were high for them also: they intended to extricate themselves from the quagmire of Vietnam under acceptable conditions and to restore vitality and confidence in the population. The best way to fulfill this dual ambition was to persuade Moscow to cease its supply of arms to Vietnam and to break new ground in establishing stable relations with the other world power.

FIRST OFFICIAL VISIT OF AN AMERICAN PRESIDENT IN MOSCOW

The Soviet and American leaders had met before. Wartime conferences had taken place between Roosevelt and Stalin, first at Teheran, then at Yalta, followed by the Potsdam conference when Truman met Stalin a few months later. Khrushchev had visited the United States in 1959; Kosygin had met with Johnson at Glassboro in 1967. Nixon, as Vice-President, had gone to the USSR in 1959. But it was the first time, in May, 1972, that a President of the United States had been invited on an official visit to the USSR. The visit planned for President Eisenhower in 1960 was canceled in the wake of the U-2 crisis. The invitation made to President Johnson, shortly before the invasion of Czechoslovakia in 1968, was turned down. In 1973, for the first time, Brezhnev made his way to the United States. Within about thirty months, in an unprecedented manner, four meetings between the leaders of the two countries were to take place. The most spectacular and fruitful of these summit talks was the first one, taking place in Moscow (May 22-30, 1972), when the first Soviet-American agreement on strategic weapons limitation was signed by the two countries, together with "Fundamental Principles of Relations," a document on the prevention of incidents on the high seas and in the airspace above them, and finally agreements on cooperation in the field of health, science and techniques, space and environment.

The Soviets, though they were enraged at the circumstances surrounding the summit, were pleased with the outcome of the meeting itself: the visit of the leader of the top world power was of great political significance. They were conscious of having acquired more prestige world-wide. It was a recognition of their power and a show of interest for what they represented: they felt flattered. The Soviet capital city was spruced up to appear at its best. Streets were cleared of rubbish, facades were renovated and some buildings in the vicinity of the Kremlin, being too decrepit, were demolished.

This trip of the American President (which was to take him to Leningrad and Kiev, after Moscow) had required patient endeavors. Early on in his term of office, he had expressed a wish to turn from confrontation to negotiation. More than three years elapsed. In 1970, he made a gesture towards meeting the Soviet leaders (in April, Kissinger had approached Ambassador Dobrynin), but nothing came of it, as the Soviets agreed in principle, but took no practical steps to follow up the proposal. A tentative date was chosen for September, 1971, but it was postponed by the Soviets, probably for tactical reasons: they hoped in return for a summit meeting to obtain concessions from the Americans, especially regarding the Berlin negotiations. Their attitude changed dramatically, according to Kissinger, after the announcement of Nixon's visit to China; immediately Dobrynin showed great eagerness to fix a date, preferably before the trip to Peking.

International problems, especially concerning Europe and the Middle East, were discussed during the meeting, but the superpowers concentrated on bilateral questions and the establishment of a new kind of relations, hence the importance given to SALT-1 and the "Basic Principles of Relations between the Soviet Union and the United States." Although the summit had been carefully prepared, when Nixon arrived in Moscow the document on strategic weapons was not ready. If an agreement was eventually reached, it was due to the fact that the leaders of the two countries were set on achieving results in this area: the exact wording of SALT-1 required long hours of negotiations (it was the main topic of discussions between the two delegations during the summit) and the task was completed only moments before the signature ceremony.

By spelling out the "Basic Principles" which were to regulate their relations, a text they signed on May 29, Richard Nixon and Leonid Brezhnev tried to adopt new terms of reference in their dealings. Their approach was dictated by the need for peaceful coexistence: they stated their belief "that in the nuclear era, there was no other basis...to support their relations," and "the differences in ideology and social systems that may exist do not hinder the development of normal relations, based on the principles of national sovereignty, equality, non-interference in internal affairs and reciprocal advantages."

Following this, they agreed a whole set of rules of conduct which they promised to respect. They stated their readiness "to do everything possible to avoid military confrontation and prevent the start of a nuclear war," to always to act "with moderation in their dealings with each other," and "to negotiate and settle differences through peaceful means." They "recognized that any attempt made by one [of the two parties] to obtain, directly or indirectly, unilateral advantages at the expense of the other, was incompatible with these objectives" and that it was their duty, and that of the other permanent members of the UN Security Council, to "do everything they could to avoid any conflict or any situation likely to increase international tension"; consequently they undertook "to try to create conditions which would enable all countries to live in peace and security, without suffering any foreign interference in their internal affairs." They also testified to their wish to cooperate in every sector. They intended to continue their exchanges and contacts at all levels, as well as developing economic, commercial, cultural, scientific and technological relations, and so on. They meant to do their best to reach agreement on arms limitations in order to make them permanent and in the end to achieve "total and general disarmament." They emphasized also that the development of relations "was not directed against third countries, nor against the interests of the latter" and that "they did not claim for themselves any right or specific advantage in world affairs."

It was the first time the superpowers had signed a document of this kind, which matched the one drafted by the PRC and the United States at the time of Nixon's visit to Peking. The two sides seemed to be in earnest about it, probably for different reasons.

The first summit enabled the leaders of both countries to establish personal contacts, open a dialogue and lay the basis of their relations for the future. This was not seen as an exceptional rence, but rather as the first in a series of regular consultations at the highest level which should allow them to keep in touch and develop cooperation.

REGULAR CONSULTATIONS AT THE HIGHEST LEVEL

When Leonid Brezhnev and Richard Nixon met again in the United States in June 18-25, 1973, they could look back on a year of close relations which had brought impressive rewards: the outline of stable coexistence had emerged; the two countries had signed more agreements than at any other period in their history, and the peace treaty on Vietnam (January, 1973), which put an end to a bitter war between the United States and an ally of the Soviet Union, had removed a serious obstacle to rapprochement.

Before his departure, the Secretary General was unsure of the reception he would get; he particularly feared demonstrations in support of Soviet Jews. Soon after arriving in the States, his apprehension vanished; he became animated, cheerful, pleasant and courteous; he appeared relaxed most of the time and even at times proved almost affectionate towards Nixon, especially in the villa of San Clemente. (The talks took place in Washington, Camp David and San Clemente.) He was very different, at least on the surface, from the person who, in 1959, had behaved in an aggressive and boastful manner; he seemed very grateful for the superb dark blue Lincoln car offered by the American government (his hosts had heard of his passion for luxury cars).

The summit had been prepared in May, at Zavidovo, by Kissinger and his assistants (Sonnenfeldt, Odeen, Hyland, Rodman and Campbell). The fact that they were entertained in this Politburo hunting lodge was a mark of distinction—no Western leader had ever been invited there—which augured well for the summit meeting.

The agreement on the prevention of nuclear war, signed on June 22 for an unlimited period, was the climax of this meeting. It was an essentially political document, a follow-up to the "Basic Principles of Relations" between the two countries. The two parties undertook to "act in such a way as to prevent the development of situations which might cause dangerously heightened tension in their relations, to avoid military confrontation and make the start of a nuclear war impossible, either between them or between one of the parties and other countries," to "abstain from resorting to threats or the use of force against the other party, against the allies of the other party or against other countries." The agreement made provisions for "urgent consultations" if "relations between the parties or between one of them and other countries seemed to indicate a risk of nuclear conflict, or if relations between non-signatory countries involved a risk of nuclear war between the USSR and the United States, or between one of the parties and other countries"—in short they would hold consultations on a wide range of situations.

This agreement, initiated by the Soviets, had been abundantly discussed, for the Americans were not in favor of the first Soviet proposals which they saw as a maneuver intended to weaken the dissuasive impact of the American nuclear "umbrella." It was in April ,1972, during a visit made by Henry Kissinger to Moscow that Brezhnev spoke for the first time of what he called "a peace bomb," a treaty banning the use of nuclear weapons; in view of the Soviet proximity to some theaters of operations such as the Middle East and Europe, this proposal could only meet with a cool reception. In the following months, the Soviet leaders raised the subject on several occasions. In May, just before the summit, Dobrynin submitted a draft treaty that the American government found impossible to accept. At the time of the meeting, when Brezhnev raised the question, Nixon reacted evasively and postponed a firm answer. The document was the subject of prolonged debate before being signed.

What was the real point of the agreement? If it aimed at setting up a system of bilateral consultations to ward off any risk of nuclear war, it was not the first of its kind. An agreement whose purpose was to prevent an accidental start to such a conflict had already been signed on September 30, 1971, in Washington: each party undertook "to warn its partner immediately of any fortuitous, illegal or unexplained incident [...] which might eventually start a nuclear war," "to give notice to its partner [...] of any launching of rockets, if these operations were conducted outside its national borders and directed at the territory of the other contracting party," and to give explanations to the other party if asked for them in the event of misunderstanding. Like the agreement which was signed on the same day whose aim was to modernize the "Red Line," it reflected the wish for better information, so as to make the position of each party clearer. In the "Basic Principles," the United States and the USSR had already committed themselves to "do their utmost to avoid military confrontation and prevent the start of nuclear war." The agreement of May 25, 1972, on the prevention of incidents on the high seas and in the airspace above them answered the same requirement. The agreement of June, 1973 put the signatory countries under no new obligation: it was not a pact of non-aggression, nor was it a ban on nuclear weapons. It did not represent a step forward on the way to disarmament, but rather another sign of political détente. It was a declaration of principles and good intentions aimed at preventing a nuclear catastrophe, expressing and legalizing the will to maintain peace and control nuclear weapons through political and diplomatic means. Yet it also expressed a new type of relations, as we shall see below.

The meeting ended with an unexpected and painful flare-up on the subject of the Middle East, the meaning of which was lost on the American leaders, according to their account. After a crowded and relaxed cocktail party, followed by a quiet dinner at Nixon's home in California, Brezhnev asked to talk to the American President who had already gone to bed. He offered to conclude a "bilateral agreement," a secret one if need be, "on a series of principles which would help to achieve a settlement in the Middle East." It would accept the withdrawal of Israel behind the 1967 borders in exchange for the end of "the state of war"; further negotiations with the Palestinians would then make peace possible. The meeting went on for three hours. As Nixon related in his memoirs, Brezhnev acted with brutal intransigence, hinting at the risk of war if the two countries did not reach an agreement. This scene coincided with a low point in the history of privileged talks. It made the Soviet conception of coexistence abundantly clear; the Soviet leaders used it as a means to share power with the United States in selected areas.

The SALT treaties were another cause for disappointment and no progress was achieved in this sector. One positive point emerged: the two parties signed a seven-points declaration, in which they promised to try to " define within a period of one year the principles of a permanent and far-reaching agreement on the limitation of offensive strategic weapons to be signed by 1974."

In the field of science and technology, cooperation was well advanced: six agreements were signed concerning agriculture, oceanography, transports, tax systems, commercial airlines and the peaceful use of nuclear power, together with a seventh one on cultural exchanges.

This second summit brought impressive results mingled with disappointments. A pattern emerged in the dialogue: attitudes had become more open but within narrow boundaries: regarding strategic and international matters, it was obvious that progress would be difficult; the fact that the interests of the two powers in some third countries (e.g., China and the Middle East) did not coincide made it difficult to find a middle ground.

The third summit (June 27-July 3, 1974) occurred one month before President Nixon was forced to resign. The Watergate affair did not prevent the Soviets giving a warm welcome to Nixon, indeed markedly warmer than the one received two years earlier. This time Brezhnev was present at the airport with Podgorny, Kosygin and Gromyko; the population was allowed to come near the officials at the airport and in the streets of Moscow, as well as in the Crimea, at Oreanda, where the talks took place.

The debate centered, as it had in the first two meetings, on negotiations for the limitation of armaments and further cooperation. A treaty on the limitation of underground tests of nuclear weapons was signed. It was decided to add further limitations concerning anti-ballistic missile systems (protocol to the 1972 treaty). A declaration regarding the intention of both parties to take measures "to eliminate any danger of using environmental means for military ends" was drafted. Several agreements were concluded in the sector of housing, medicine, energy, economic, industrial and technical cooperation.

The international questions primarily addressed the Middle East and Europe: in the final communiqué, the two parties stated their desire that "the final stage of the Conference on European security take place shortly" and deemed the "results of negotiations to be such as to permit a conclusion of the conference at the highest level." The Soviets, who attached great importance to it, were delighted.

The meeting between Brezhnev and President Ford at Vladivostok on November 23-24, 1974, was the last summit, but it did not appear as such at the time: the two leaders touched on Brezhnev's visit to the United States in 1975. Both sides stressed that a change in the Administration should have no harmful effect on the pursuit of détente. The Soviets were favorably impressed by the new American President's promise, in his first address to Congress, to continue Nixon's Soviet policy.

The main outcome of this mini-summit (negotiations lasted only a day and a half) was something that had been talked about for several months on the subject of limitation of offensive strategic weapons: a preliminary agreement to the negotiations for a final draft, prepared by Kissinger during his Moscow visit of October, 1974, was signed. Discussions on the world situation focused mainly on the Middle East. The Soviets were worried about American advances in the region (at their expense) and advocated a settlement in which the two great powers would participate. The final communiqué referred to the Palestinian people and a conference in Geneva, which the Soviets had insisted upon, seemed to placate them, but it was worded in such a vague manner as to leave the Americans uncommitted.

The fact that the leaders of the two great powers made a point of meeting at regular intervals to analyze world affairs, to hold consultations and to strengthen relations had great political significance, although the talks failed to bring about all the effects that had been hoped for. The face-to-face nature of these exchanges and their occurrence at regular intervals gave them an impact capable of changing the course of history and proved to the whole world how important was the continuation of dialogue.

INCREASE IN BILATERAL RELATIONS

The main change in relations between the two countries was not only introduced by these summit meetings, but above all through routine exchanges in many areas. Between 1971 and 1974, many government members stayed repeatedly in Moscow: Kissinger, the national security advisor, who became Secretary of State on August 23, 1973; his predecessor, W. Rogers; the trade secretary, M. Stans, and his successors, P. Peterson and M. Dent; the Agriculture secretary, E. Butz; the Treasury secretary, G. Shultz and his successor, W. Simon; the Health secretary, G. Weinberger, and so forth. Their Soviet counterparts, the Foreign Minister, A. Gromyko; the minister for foreign trade, N. Patolichev and several deputy-ministers for foreign trade, V. Alkhimov, M. Manyulo, N. Smelyakov; the Transport minister, B. Beshchev; the Merchant Navy minister, T. Guzhenko; the First chief deputy-commander of the Navy, V. Kasatonov; the Civil Aviation minister, Bugaev; the minister for Irrigation and Water Management, E. Alexeiev; the Culture minister, E. Furtseva; the Health minister, B. Petrovskij—all flocked to the United States. M.P.s and local representatives of both countries also developed close relations. Senators Muskie, Scott, Humphrey, Bellmon, Hartke, Kennedy, the chairman of the House of Representatives, Albert, and the mayors of New York and San Francisco were entertained in the USSR, while a delegation of the Supreme Soviet headed by B. Ponomarev, as well as the Mayor of Moscow, went to the United States.

American businessmen and their bank managers traveled to the Soviet Union to study the possibilities offered by a new market, including H. Ford, A. Hammer, chairman of Occidental Petroleum, D. Kendall, chairman of PepsiCo and of the Soviet-American Chamber of Commerce, T. Watson, chairman of IBM, H. Kearns, chairman of American bank of Import-Export and many others. The Chase Manhattan Bank, the Bank of America and the first National City Bank opened branches in Moscow. According to the American press, in 1973 some 300 businessmen a week stayed in Moscow compared to some fifty in the previous year.

Scientific and technical cooperation was also abundantly discussed. The President and Deputy President of the Science Academy of the USSR, M. Keldysh and M. Millionshchikov, as well as the President and Deputy President of the State Committee for Science and Techniques, V. Kirillin and A. Trapeznikov, stayed in the United States, and the President of the National Science Academy of the United States, Dr. Handler, and the head of NASA, Dr. Fletcher, visited the USSR.

Mixed commissions, together with conferences in which both sides participated, round tables, exhibitions and fairs in many different sectors, became common occurrences in the new climate.

Communications between the two countries improved as exchanges multiplied. After the "Red Line" had been established in 1963, the two parties agreed to set up another two in 1969, one to link the American Embassy in Moscow to the Department of State and the other connecting the Soviet Embassy in Washington to the Foreign Ministry of the USSR. On September 30, 1971, measures to upgrade the Red Line's efficiency were taken. An agreement on air connections, in November, 1966, established a direct line Moscow-New York. In 1970, it was decided to open a new line, Anchorage (Alaska)-Khabarovsk (Siberia), planned to be in operation only in the summer months. In June, 1973, another agreement made for further increase in air traffic: more flights and lines would be available; Pan American Airlines started a New York-Leningrad line and Aeroflot a Moscow-Washington one. In 1973, a Soviet Consulate general was inaugurated in San Francisco and an American consulate in Leningrad, showing that the two countries meant to increase contacts.

In 1969, the beginning of another direct connection between the White House and the Kremlin, via the Soviet Embassy in Washington, marked an important development in communications. Regular meetings between Kissinger and Ambassador Dobrynin, at a minimum of a monthly interval, on an official or sometimes unofficial footing, allowed the two governments to exchange their views in an informal fashion and to find out about each other's intentions, thus avoiding being bogged down by administrative delays. The fact that Dobrynin could enter the White House freely, without having to show his credentials, that he left his car in the private car-park of the State Department and used the private lift of the Secretary of State, making his visit as discrete as possible, demonstrated the new climate of improved relations between the two countries and the wish of the leaders for greater efficiency.

DÉTENTE AT THE TIME OF WATERGATE

The balance of power between the two countries shifted considerably in the period 1972 to 1974. Because of this, summit meetings were not all of equal importance. As Nixon gradually lost his grip on power, negotiations reflected the altered situation. If the American President had enjoyed the same degree of influence in 1974 as two years earlier, results would undoubtedly have been more impressive. The many new problems arising in 1973 would have been examined in a cooler manner and solutions might have been found. Debate on strategic questions might have made some progress, but as one month followed another, the gap became wider between Soviet leaders who insisted on détente and an American Administration increasingly absorbed by internal problems.

From the time of the second summit, the Watergate affair loomed large in the talks between the two countries. On this occasion, the Soviet delegation could observe at close range the harm done by the scandal. The situation in the United States was so uncertain that one can only wonder what impact it had on détente. President Nixon's position was even then very shaky. Henry Kissinger gave April, 1973, as the month when he gave up all hope of seeing the Administration emerge from the Watergate affair and politics resume a "normal" course (*The Stormy Years*, pp. 115-6), that is to say, at least two months before the summit. It would be surprising if the Soviets had taken no notice of the weakened position of the American President, especially since on the day Brezhnev departed—June 25—Congress approved a draft law of the Senate which cut credits allowed for US bombing in Cambodia. Nixon had opposed this, and it heralded a series of decisions which would deprive the American government of all means of putting pressure on North Vietnam, i.e., of ensuring that the Paris peace agreements would be respected.

The third summit, one month before President Nixon's resignation, took place in circumstances even more unfavorable. Curiously, it did not appear as completely untimely to the Americans: 52% of the people consulted before Richard Nixon left thought the meeting should have been canceled (Louis Harris poll), which is a small proportion considering how weak he was by then. The Soviet leaders must have been aware at the time that their partner had little room to maneuver. Why did they want to talk to him? Did they expect him, all the same, to clear his name finally and stay in power until 1976? Did American successes on the international scene, especially in the Middle East (e.g., Kissinger's step by step policy, rapprochement between the US and Egypt) encourage them in this belief, in spite of the internal difficulties of the President?

It is clear that the Soviets felt uneasy, not only because of Watergate but also because the talks were already in trouble. Yet the trip was still on, and the Soviet press claimed that the objective was to turn these summits into routine meetings which would take place at regular intervals and breathe new life into the process of détente. The proposal made by Brezhnev to Nixon during a private conversation for a mutual assistance pact (an idea already suggested in July, 1970 by M. Semenov, head of the Soviet delegation to the SALT talks) demonstrates that the USSR put privileged dialogue high on their list of priorities. The fact that they did not change course in spite of all the problems shows they still hoped to benefit from the operation.

The efforts made on both sides to normalize relations did not stop at politics. What was remarkable in the new climate was the way the leaders tried to control rivalries and put exchanges on a regular basis.

3

DÉTENTE: ARMS CONTROL

In an unprecedented gesture, the superpowers got together to negotiate an effective limitation in armament building, based on a formal agreement. This development was both a matter of strategy and politics.

All agreements thus far reached by the two countries aimed at curbing nuclear weapons proliferation worldwide, either by setting geographical boundaries to "horizontal" growth, as was the case with treaties on the Antarctica (1959), of Tlatelolco (1967), on space beyond the earth's atmosphere (1967), on keeping the sea free of nuclear devices (1971), thereby preserving certain areas from the arms race, or attempting to limit third countries' future advances. Immediately after the Cuba crisis, the two great powers concluded a treaty establishing a partial ban on nuclear testing (August 5, 1963) and on July 1, 1968, they signed the treaty of nuclear non-proliferation. These two documents opened the way to armament control and showed that the interests of the two powers could sometimes coincide, but they mostly concerned third countries. The 1963 treaty dealt with the kind of tests that the great powers no longer needed technically: the possibility of underground testing was still open (it is still operative). The important point was not so much that they gave up anything, but rather they tried to impose a ban on countries still in need of this kind of experimentation. The 1968 treaty, in which the parties declared themselves in favor of measures to reduce stockpiles of nuclear weapons, did not affect their own forces decisively.

The possibility of disarmament was considered on many occasions, but proposals in this direction (the US-Soviet declaration of September 20, 1961, for example) remained fruitless. The same thing happened to various propositions intended to create a climate of trust, like that of "open skies" put forward by President Eisenhower on July 21, 1955.

The notion of the great powers negotiating armament control for their own side had been raised, but without success. The Soviets refused an offer made by President Johnson, on January 21, 1964, of a freeze on nuclear weapons: they did not wish to negotiate from the inferior position they found themselves in at the time.

31

Yet, after the Cuban crisis, when the risk of direct confrontation between the superpowers became clear, there was a change in attitude. Competition went hand in hand, as was seen above, with an attempt at establishing a dialogue which took shape in the red telephone line and the treaty on a partial ban of nuclear testing. In these circumstances the idea emerged, not of disarmament, but of arms *control*, in order to lessen the danger and to preserve the nuclear balance. On January 27, 1967, President Johnson offered to renew negotiations. The American leaders, worrying about the Soviet advances in the field of defensive weapons, especially the setting up of the Galosh ring round Moscow, (which soon turned out to have been overestimated) and being under pressure from Congress, were keen to open talks on this subject. Although the Soviets responded by an article in *Pravda* of February 15, 1967, in which they declared their readiness to negotiate, it took them almost 18 months to consent to it: on June 27, 1968, Andrei Gromyko announced in front of the Supreme Soviet that his country accepted the American proposal to start discussions on the limitation and reduction of strategic weapons and that he agreed to talks covering both defensive and offensive armament.

Three days later, on July 1, 1968, the day the treaty of non-proliferation was signed, the US and the USSR announced their decision to start discussions. The Soviet intervention in Czecho-slovakia (August 1968) delayed the opening of negotiations that the Soviets had repeatedly called for (they had proposed, for example, to begin before the new American President was sworn in on January 20, 1969). On November 17, 1969, the Helsinki talks finally began, after the new Republican Administration had had time to think the matter over. Both Congress and public opinion approved this decision. The negotiations, officially led by G.C. Smith on the American side and V. Semenov on the Soviet side, took place alternately in Helsinki and Vienna over two and a half years until on May 26, 1972, after many false starts, the first agreement on the limitation of strategic weapons was signed.

If the Soviets were now willing to change their minds, it was because the situation was very different from what it had been a few years earlier. During the 1960s, to catch up with their American rivals they had made a sustained effort which had produced impressive results. Late in 1964, a decision was made to develop intercontinental ballistic missiles (ICBM) as a matter of urgency; a huge increase in the number of missiles based on sub-marines (SLBM) followed from

1968 onwards; a defensive anti-missile system was launched, probably early in the decade; by 1960-62, the Americans discovered that the Soviets were starting to deploy an ABM system round Leningrad, and, in November 1964, at the time of the parade to celebrate the anniversary of the Revolution, they saw the first ABM missiles. The Soviet strategic capability which in 1965 amounted to some 220 ICBMs and 100 SLBMs, had risen, three years later, to some 860 ICBMs and 120 SLBMs.

Around that time, the United States, in view of its marked superiority over the USSR, decided to put a ceiling on the number of ICBMs and SLBMs and to stop production of strategic bombers, that is to say, to keep their strategic capability at the same level (1054 ICBMs, 656 SLBMs, and about 400 B-52 bomber aircraft), while improving their rockets (making them more accurate, less vulnerable and equipped with multiple warheads).

Early in the 1970s, a kind of equilibrium between the superpowers was reached. The Americans still had a qualitative advantage, particularly because of the MIRV (these multiple heads missiles were first tested in the air in 1968 and became operational in June 1970) and the Soviets did not have the technical capacity then to have them—they had only developed MRV, multiple head rockets which could not be guided independently from one another. Yet as regards quantity, because the Americans, due to the reluctance of Congress and public opinion (it was the height of the Vietnam crisis), had delayed the start of various modernization programs that had been planned for their strategic weapons (such as the B1 bomber aircraft and Trident submarine) while the Soviets carried on with their armament drive, the latter were no longer disadvantaged but a balance had been established and, in some sectors, they were leading (especially in the number of ICBM launchers). Soviet advances and the heady feeling of being able to exert pressure on American strategic programs at the negotiating table incited them to accept some limitation on their forces.

The determining factor in achieving success, in this matter as in the others, was the political will shown by both parties to achieve results. Each time the talks got bogged down, preference was given to political means over the technical side: any difficulty was referred to the leaders of both countries. The official negotiations taking place in Helsinki and Vienna were, in any case, practically always reciprocated by direct exchanges via Kissinger and Dobrynin; sometimes the negotiators themselves were unaware of them.

The matter of a connection between offensive and defensive systems was the main problem to settle. It was vital to deal with it since they both were essential to dissuasion. The reprisals brought about by a nuclear attack prevented each of the superpowers from taking the initiative and attacking: the advantage gained by the aggressor would be canceled by the other party's reaction. Dissuasion, to be effective, required that neither of them should be in possession of a network of defensive weapons which would allow one to substantially ward off the other's reprisals; neither should one enjoy an offensive capability enabling him to annihilate, at a first strike, a proportion of the other's nuclear potential so large that the latter would not be in a position to react efficiently, that is to say, inflicting damages deemed intolerable to the aggressor.

Originally, in 1967, the Americans were uneasy because of the Galosh network and wished to keep the matter of defensive weapons as the main subject for discussions. The Soviets, on the contrary, preferred to talk about offensive weapons at the time. In 1970, it was the opposite. The Americans, due to Soviet advances in intercontinental missiles, focused their attention on limitation of offensive weapons, while the Soviets, probably disappointed with the costly and inefficient ABM systems as well as apprehensive of American development of an anti-missile network which would perform much better than their own, concentrated on defensive weapons. They were still willing to hold talks on offensive systems, but separately. Added to this was the difficulty of pinpointing the offensive weapons which would come under consideration; it was therefore necessary to define which would be called "strategic." The Soviets considered that any nuclear weapon capable of reaching the other's territory qualified as strategic. Such a definition was not acceptable to the Americans, since it allowed the Soviets to include in the negotiation all American tactical weapons based abroad, in Europe especially, and on the contrary to rule out their Soviet counterparts which threatened Europe but could not reach US territory. What Washington suggested was to deal with intercontinental weapons according to their geographical range (over 5,500 km) not the place in which they were located. In 1971, negotiations got bogged down because of these difficulties, but in the end they were overcome through a political compromise. On May 20, 1971, the leaders of the two countries found an arrangement to resume negotiations: they decided to preserve a link between defensive and offensive devices, to focus discussions on the areas of agreement, i.e., drafting a treaty limiting defensive weapons and freezing some offensive strategic armaments, while other problems would be addressed at a later date.

Occasionally specific problems at the center of debate were handled during summit meetings. The role played by the political authorities became prominent when the time came for signing agreements: the last difficulties were ironed out at Moscow, not by negotiators, but by Nixon, Brezhnev and their advisors (Smirnov, Gromyko, Alexandrov, Dobrynin and Kornienko on the Soviet side, and Kissinger, Sonnenfeldt, Hyland and Lord on the American side).

On March 26, 1972, two and a half years of negotiations were concluded in Moscow with the signing of a Treaty on limitation of antiballistic missile systems and a temporary agreement concerning measures intended to limit offensive strategic weapons.

Would it have been possible to reach such an agreement if the leaders had not taken part themselves in the various stages of negotiations, especially in the final one, and if the international situation (Soviet fears of a rapprochement between China and the US and Washington's desire to gain Soviet assistance in order to end the Vietnam war) had not forced the leaders of the two countries to seek a compromise? One wonders, since SALT-1 was obviously "handled" as part of a wide political agreement intended to facilitate privileged relations between the superpowers.

FINAL LIMITATION OF DEFENSIVE WEAPONS

The ABM treaty, valid for an unlimited period, in principle put a limitation to the development of defensive weapons: the two countries would no longer try to defend the national territory, either in its entirety or partially, except for two sites (later to be reduced to one).

From the mid-1950s, to counteract Soviet advances in missile building, the Americans had started researching into anti-missile defense. The aim was to detect enemy missiles by means of radar and to intercept them with rockets so as to protect the civilian population or the supreme command from outside aggression. In 1966, when they found out about the Galosh system surrounding Moscow (the Leningrad-based one seemed to have been suspended), they decided to develop an ABM system. In September 1967, McNamara announced the installation of a program called Sentinel. Such a decision attracted much criticism. Congressmen judged the program to be either excessive or insufficient—all doubted that the Soviet threat was being countered. American scientific circles did not believe the technical capacity existed. The controversy made Richard Nixon reconsider the decision, on his arrival at the White House: in March 1969, he chose instead the Safeguard Program. In 1972, two of the twelve sites selected for this program were almost completed: Grand Forks in North Dakota and Malmstrom in Montana.

The development of an anti-missile defense had far-reaching consequences, as was seen above, on the doctrine of reciprocal vulnerability and therefore of dissuasion. It also had an effect on the arms race, since it encouraged the adversary either to try to acquire a defensive system more spread out in order to be protected from enemy attack, or to set up new offensive weapons capable of over-coming the other's defense. In this sense it was largely destabilizing. The changes occurring in arms programs on either side were not due to a single factor (there is an in-built dynamism in research projects), but they depended partly on the other's advances. American superiority was one of the reasons for the decision of the Soviets to develop an ABM defense system, and in turn this system (much less sophisticated than the Americans had thought to start with) drove the latter to launch the Sentinel and later Safeguard programs in spite of shortcomings and high cost, and to embark on the development of MRV and finally MIRV.

With the new treaty freezing existing programs, the Nixon Administration was certain of having achieved limitation in the defensive weapons race and having preserved the validity of the concept of dissuasion by mutual terror: both undertook not to try to put out of action the other's capability for retaliation. Since they were no longer in a position either fully or even partially to defend their territory and population against a nuclear attack, it was imperative to prevent a first strike which would destroy them. This situation seemed highly satisfactory and the news of the treaty was favorably received in the United States: it was approved by the Senate on August 3, 1972, with 88 votes against 2, almost unanimously.

According to the wording of the treaty, after committing themselves not to develop anti-missile defense systems to protect their territory, the two countries agreed to limit their defense to two sites, with a maximum radius of 150 km, one around the capital of each party, the other covering a zone equipped with silos for ICBM launchers, each site not containing more than 100 launchers, 100 intercepting missiles, and a limited number of radar stations. This definition was harsh for the Americans since they were obliged to dismantle one of the two sites then almost completed (Malmstrom was abandoned). To avoid the risk of the two sites that were allowed being combined to form a defensive core covering a whole region or the entire territory, it was stated in a separate paragraph to be initialed that the two sites had to be situated at a distance of no less than 1,300 km. All ABM systems or component parts "based at sea, in the air, in space or on mobile land platforms" were forbidden and each party "undertook not to transfer to other states, nor to deploy outside its national territory ABM systems or components which are subject to limitation under the terms of the treaty." Nevertheless, research in this field was permitted, which augured badly for the future; within the limits of the treaty's dispositions, ABM systems or their components could be modernized or replaced (verification problems would arise if this was not the case). Ten years later, it appeared that progress in research carried out after 1972 radically altered the situation.

Initially, the negotiations which continued after the 1972 summit proved positive: two years later, at the time of a third summit, both parties agreed to improve on the existing arrangements and keep only one of the two anti-missile sites allowed in the 1972 document. In 1977, summing up past achievements in this area, the Americans were genuinely satisfied with the way the treaty had been applied.

The Soviets had every reason to congratulate themselves, as the American program, much more dynamic and advanced than their own, was interrupted. The reason the Americans accepted this limitation was not only to put an end to the defensive weapons race but also to impose on the Soviets a limitation of their offensive weapons.

A PARTIAL AND TEMPORARY FREEZE OF OFFENSIVE WEAPONS

The interim accord was much more limited in its action: it was valid only for five years, unless it was "replaced before this time expired by an agreement bearing on more extensive measures" and concerned only certain weapons: ICBMs, SLBMs and nuclear submarines equipped with SLBMs. The ICBMs concerned were the land-based non-movable missiles with a range exceeding 5,500 km (the distance between the western border of the USSR and the Eastern coast of the United States). The agreement did not cover mobile land ICBMs; it did not take into account the number of nuclear heads; it did not include either strategic bomber aircraft or middle or intermediary range missiles, nor in principle American FBS (Forward Based Systems). In reality it seems that the FBS factor played an important part in the negotiations—it represented a problem still to be solved: the Soviets explicitly stated at the time of signing that they would reopen the debate later. Besides, these bases were probably taken into consideration when working out a strategic balance.

It was not a disarmament agreement, not even a reduction in armament: it was a freeze of certain specific weapons. First of all ICBMs: the construction of new land-based launching pads was ruled out after July 1, 1972. Within these limits, modernization and replacement of the ICBMs were allowed, but the two parties undertook not to convert the land-based launching pads for light caliber ICBMs or older-type ICBMs designed before 1964 into launching pads for heavy land-based ICBMs of a more recent type, i.e., not to change first generation devices into second generation ICBMs. The distinction between ICBMs built before 1964 and those built later was intended to prevent the Soviets continuing their development of heavy missiles capable of taking large loads, which once they were provided with multiple heads would threaten the survival of American ICBMs.

There was no precise figure, either in the document or in the accompanying protocol, on the number of ICBMs available to each country. In spite of American pressure, the Soviet side refused to reveal its capacity. The United States therefore declared unilaterally that, at the time of signing, they had 1,054 ICBMs and the Soviets 1,618 of which 313 were heavy ICBMs (SS-9 or missiles of a similar type), a declaration indirectly confirmed by the USSR since it did not object. Out of these, according to the Americans, 1,550 were operational, including 288 heavy ICBMs, while the others were near completion (launchers being built could become operational, which applied to the Soviet ones only, since there were none in the pipeline on the American).

As regards the SLBMs and modern ballistic submarines, the two parties were committed to limit them "to the number, on the one hand, of those that are operational or being built at the date of signing" of the agreement, and "on the other hand to the amount of launchers and submarines built to replace the same number of ICBM launchers of an older type, built before 1964, or launchers installed on board older submarines." Concerning these weapons, precise figures were given, not in the agreement, but in its protocol. A first ceiling for the USSR was set at 740 launchers on nuclear submarines of all categories (in active service or being built) and for the United States at 656 (all operational). Another limitation could be reached under certain circumstances, following a complicated system of exchanges between several categories of weapons: the United States were entitled to possess up to 710 launchers and 44 submarines, the USSR up to 950 launchers and 62 submarines, if they destroyed beyond these numbers an equal number of ICBM launchers of a pre-1964 type or of SLBM launchers placed on older submarines. This complexity was due to the fact that the United States did not have older submarines comparable to the Soviet ones, that the Soviets had submarines with either 12 or 16 launchers, and also that the two parties could not agree during the negotiations on the number of modern Soviet nuclear submarines: the Soviets claimed 48, while the Americans estimated a mere 41-43.

The first characteristic of this agreement was imbalance in numbers: the USSR was allowed a larger number of ICBMs, SLBMs and nuclear submarines than the United States. Such inequality aroused bitter criticism in the United States as soon as the terms were made public, as it was thought that, apart from other considerations, its psychological impact on the American population might lead to an inferiority complex. The Administration justified the decision on the grounds that the United States, unlike the USSR, had no program of development for new ICBMs, nor new types of submarines being built: the agreement, it was explained, put a brake on the increase in Soviet armaments which would have been much higher if no limitation had been set, while the United States, in any case, would not have carried out any modernization program between 1972 and 1977. Military specialists later blamed the leadership for this attitude. Yet as Kissinger pointed out, at the time the document was signed, each year the Soviets built 250 ICBMs, 128 SLBMs and 8 submarines: at this rate, without the freeze, they would have 90 submarines at their disposal after five years. In view of these figures the agreement made sense, in his opinion. The advantage in numbers seems to have also been a way of compensating the Soviet side for leaving the FBS out of the account. This is one explanation of the declaration made by Kissinger on May 27, 1972.

This reasoning did not satisfy certain sectors of public opinion which wished to preserve American superiority. Nixon was accused of neglecting the needs of American security. The memory of many years of anti-communist struggle explained this sharp reaction.

Public opinion was so accustomed to believe all decisions made by the USSR were influenced by a strong antagonism to the United States that it found it difficult to imagine anything else. Moreover, these questions were highly technical and beyond most people's understanding. In Congress, some personalities, like Senators Goldwater and Jackson, violently attacked this numerical imbalance. The latter had an amendment passed to the effect that, in future negotiations, the government would defend the principle of parity.

The criticism had to be seen as a political fact, although the anxiety it revealed was not very rational. Numerical imbalance by itself, as the Administration pointed out, was hardly disquieting when the agreement was signed, in view of the large technological advantage of the Americans in other sectors not covered by the deal (MIRV, heavy bomber aircraft, nuclear heads, etc.). If of necessity qualitative factors are taken into account, nuclear parity is extremely difficult to achieve, the forces in balance being asymmetrical and geographical as well as political situations being widely different. It was an argument put forward by the Soviets to have the Americans recognize their right to possess higher strategic forces. The substantial advantage enjoyed by the USSR in 1972, in relation to the United States regarding missile weight, so long as missiles were not "mirved," could not be considered as decisive. In the long and middle term, this discrepancy was on the other hand very worrying, since the Soviets could make rapid technological advances. But it soon proved nonsensical in any case because of the widely varying interpretation given to it by both sides. The Soviets saw it as the Americans acknowledging their right to have, for an unlimited period, a number of launchers and weight-bearing capability much higher than their own, while the United States believed the agreement to be a temporary freeze of certain weapons which, together with the ABM treaty would set the necessary conditions for signing a more balanced and wider accord on offensive weapons in the near future; they considered SALT-1 possible only because SALT-2 would remedy its shortcomings. This imbalance, though it was more apparent than real, represented a problem which the Americans became fully aware of in later months. It was clear even then that the definition of parity was finally the main stumbling-block in the negotiations.

The interim agreement was unsatisfactory, not so much because of this imbalance as because the whole range of weapons was not covered. The arms race was frozen in certain limited areas, but it could continue elsewhere. In other words, it did not slow down but merely shifted to another sector. Taking into account only the number of launchers but not the heads was a boost for research into miniaturization and precision in weapons, and this new direction, ten years later, forced a reappraisal of SALT-1. This first agreement was a necessary step on the way to arms control and was a positive sign of determination to slow down the arms race and stabilize the nuclear balance. Yet it should be remembered that the most intractable problems were put aside at the time. This is why the interim agreement gave rise to a much more heated debate than the ABM treaty did. Its approval by Congress was more difficult to obtain than approval for the treaty.

One of the reasons why it was impossible to make further progress was the Soviet refusal to allow verification on the spot. The ABM treaty and the interim agreement covered areas where verification could be carried out through national technical means, mostly thanks to observation satellites. It was a sophisticated means of control, but not unlimited: the number of nuclear heads carried, the range and capacity of the nuclear weapons could be assessed only by testing. As for the agreements signed thus far, the Americans thought the means of verification were adequate, in view of the fact that each party was bound not to thwart the work of the other's controllers and a permanent consultative Commission was appointed. These clauses attracted criticism also. People like Andrei Sakharov found them quite insufficient for both offensive and defensive weapons.

The achievements of SALT-1 were more significant in the field of defensive weapons from the point of view of the USSR, as it obtained the limitation of the American program, which was vastly more advanced and dynamic than its own, while the United States benefited in the area of offensive weapons (limitation of ballistic missiles on submarines, but above all of Soviet ICBMs) and believed the problem of load-carrying capability of these missiles had been solved. This goes some way to explain why the treaty and the agreement were not seen as separate. The negotiators linked them together by making it conditional that the convention would be applied only after the treaty was ratified and after explicit recognition of the interaction of offensive and defensive weapons (mentioned in the preamble to the treaty). At the time of signing, Henry Kissinger made it clear that the American government had serious doubts, not without reason, of the treaty remaining operative if further negotiations on offensive weapons ended in failure.

Despite all the criticism concerning the numerical advantage granted to the Soviets in the interim agreement, public opinion reacted rather favorably to SALT-1. Though the Americans were disturbed by the decisions outlined in the agreement on offensive weapons, they were happy to see their government move towards armaments control.

Even if it fell short of expectations, SALT-1 represented a major achievement which the leaders of the two countries celebrated enthusiastically. It was signed in May 1972, at the height of the Vietnam crisis and was both a strategic and political victory, clearly showing where Soviet priorities lay, demonstrating that the super-powers had joint interests, and enabling the United States to make the difficulties encountered in Vietnam seem less of a threat. It had great political significance, since for the first time the Americans did not display any superiority in their attitude.

FROM SUPERIORITY TO PARITY

With the Cuban crisis the position of the United States changed. The need to preserve stability became paramount. Simultaneously, the Americans had no wish to give up their advantage in the strategic field. On October 24, 1968, Nixon declared himself favorable to overall superiority. He denounced the Democratic Party's aim of parity and promised to defend his side's superiority, though he would not take each sector separately or each category of armament, but consider the global picture, which was an tacit admission that overall superiority could be compatible with inferiority in some aspects of defense. In January 1969, when the President gave his first press conference at the White House, he advocated sufficiency, the objective being to ensure adequate military power for the United States to protect their interests and fulfill their engagements. (Nixon often used the word "sufficiency" in the following months and years.) In his Brussels declaration of April 10, 1969, at a NATO conference, in which he described the West as no longer enjoying the massive nuclear predominance it once had at a time when an arms agreement with the Soviet Union to codify the existing balance would have been desirable, he clearly showed that parity had become acceptable.

Later on, Nixon made his position more explicit and revealed its ambiguity: it appeared that he did not see much difference between the notion of superiority, sufficiency and parity—in other words, the political line had altered compared to the previous one, but not in a radical way. According to the new doctrine which he explained was both defensive and realistic, in so far as it acknowledged the changes in power relations, the United States could put up with certain numerical advantages granted to the Soviets, but on the other hand they could not tolerate overall superiority. It more or less implied that qualitatively the objective was to preserve superiority. "No power on earth is to-day stronger than the United States. And none will be so. It is the only policy of national defense ever acceptable for the United States," Nixon declared to Congress on June 1 after returning from Moscow. These words were intended to reassure American public opinion. The latter was so used to superiority that accepting parity was not easy and appeared to be a threat and an humiliation for the United States.

This new vocabulary, though rather imprecise, was of great importance, as it revealed a change in mentality which in the long term might be capable of influencing the American perception of the Soviet Union and, even more hopeful, the Soviet vision of the United States and the world balance of forces. The fact that parity had been the basis for negotiations and the agreements that had been signed, that equality between the two countries, that is to say the end of American supremacy, had been acknowledged in the documents, was very significant.

SALT-1: A STEP TOWARDS STRATEGIC BALANCE

In SALT-1, the United States and the USSR committed themselves "to continue active negotiations on the limitation of offensive strategic armaments...in order to conclude an agreement as soon as possible" in this sector. This hope turned out to be difficult to realize. Negotiations had resumed by November 1972. The first session, lasting one month, ended with the establishment, on December 21, of a permanent consultative commission (whose task was to enforce the application of the dispositions of SALT-1 and of the September 30, 1971, agreement). It was decided that the commission would meet at least twice a year and whenever one of the parties would require it, but it also made obvious the fact that the problems remained the same as before and that an agreement on offensive weapons would not be reached easily. This was confirmed by subsequent meetings. The only result brought about by the second summit was a declaration of intent: the two parties stated again the desirability of new measures for limitation in strategic offensive weapons. They indicated that the latter would be based on the respect of equal security and could be quantitative as well as qualitative in nature. There was one precise element: the two parties undertook to try to "define within a year the principles of a permanent agreement on more far-reaching measures of limitation in the field of offensive strategic weapons so as to sign it in 1974."

On September 25, 1973, negotiations resumed in Geneva. The new proposals of the USSR (contained in a 21-point plan), which demanded, among other things, the disappearance of American forward systems and that other nuclear powers' potential would be taken into consideration to work out new ceilings, did not help to find a way out of difficulties. At the time of the third summit, the two sides made some progress in two directions: defensive weapons —as mentioned above, each went down from two ABM zones to one, the United States giving precedence to the area of silos of ICBM launchers while the USSR preferred to protect the capital—and nuclear tests, with the signing on July 3, 1974, of a Treaty on the limitation of underground testing for nuclear weapons, for a duration of five years. Under the terms of this treaty, which was a follow-up to the 1963 one (though this later treaty was bilateral), from March 31, 1976, the two sides were bound not to carry out underground testing over 150 kilotons. This limitation did not prevent the superpowers from improving the accuracy of their weapons; the two-year delay made it possible for them to go ahead with current programs. Under the terms of the accompanying protocol, the parties were to exchange a number of data which had been kept secret up to then (geographical coordinates of the area of testing, geological information concerning the zones where tests were carried out, etc.), and which were necessary to enforce control of the treaty. Two years later (March 28, 1976) another treaty was added concerning nuclear underground testing for peaceful uses.

At the third summit, the two parties issued a joint declaration in which they agreed to refrain from using any environmental means to military ends. Yet on the question of offensive weapons no advance was made. The two sides stated the need for an agreement on this point, but did not envisage signing it before the end of the year, neither did they hope to make it permanent: when it was signed, the treaty "should cover the period from that time until 1985" (joint declaration).

At Vladivostok, on November 23 and 24, 1974, President Gerald Ford and Leonid Brezhnev, in a desperate attempt to keep earlier promises, arrived at a preliminary agreement which made it possible to start further negotiations. The new convention, to be signed in the near future it was hoped, perhaps during Brezhnev's visit to the United States in 1975, was to renew the dispositions of the 1972 interim agreement (valid until 1977) and cover the period from October 1977 to December 1985. Based on the principle of equality and equal security, it would impose on each of the two great powers an overall ceiling of 2,400 strategic weapons (ICBMs, SLBMs, and bomber aircraft), 1,320 of these devices possibly equipped with MIRV, and within these limits each was free to choose whichever type of weapons he preferred. This pre-agreement was vital to the Americans: in the summer of 1973 the Soviets had successfully experimented with their first MIRV. American experts were afraid therefore that the numerical advantage granted to the Soviet side might threaten the survival of the whole land component of the American strategic force (ICBMs) because of improved accuracy and efficiency, and therefore give the adversary the possibility of dealing a " first strike." (The US at the time had 1,054 ICBMs, 656 SLBMs and 437 bomber aircraft, a total of 2,147 nuclear carriers, and the USSR had 1,575 ICBMs, 720 SLBMs and 140 bomber aircraft, a total of 2,435 carriers.) This agreement, insofar as the two countries were returning to the principle of equal numbers, seemed satisfactory. Yet this achievement had its reverse side since the arrangement practically gave a free rein to the USSR in the development of its MIRV program (high limits had been set) and did not take into account the problem of load capacity of the new Soviet missiles (which could be "mirved" also). Furthermore, the question of verification of limitation on MIRVs had not been solved. It was an advance on SALT-1, but the situation remained potentially unstable because of a marked imbalance in capability between the two sides, a phenomenon which was not helped by the rapid technological progress of the USSR.

This agreement, though it was fully approved—without reservations, as usual—by the Politburo, by the Presidium of the Supreme Soviet and the Council of Ministers of the USSR, was immediately the butt of sharp criticism in the United States. The government was blamed for putting too high a ceiling on all weapons and MIRVs especially, for not attempting to achieve reductions (the agreement only allowed for "new negotiations by 1980-81 at the latest and fresh limitations and possible reductions in strategic weapons in the period after 1985"), for not taking into consideration technological and qualitative aspects, which appeared more and more as grounds for competition, for failing to deal with serious problems, such as the emergence of "new weapons" (Backfire type Soviet bomber aircraft and Cruise missiles), etc.—in short, for entering into an essentially "political" agreement to avoid letting the Soviets keep their numerical advantage. American reactions were so heated and the unsolved problems so complicated that further prolonged negotiations were necessary to reach an agreement. SALT-2 was not signed in 1975, nor even in 1977 when SALT-1 expired, but only in 1979.

Any hope for real arms control that had arisen from SALT-1 seemed already difficult to fulfill. The strategic policy conducted by the Soviets puzzled the Americans. There was no consensus in the US on the aims of the USSR in the SALT negotiations and thus determining a policy was difficult. Competitiveness, instead of slowing down, seemed to accelerate as the two powers directed their efforts towards areas not covered by the agreement (e.g., new programs and technological innovations), which was likely to alter significantly the strategic balance. As soon as SALT-1 was signed, the Nixon Administration asked Congress for increased credits in order to push forward certain strategic programs (Trident submarine, B-1 bomber aircraft, etc.) whose deployment appeared urgent. It was not easy to see the logic behind this request for increased military expenditure at a time when a treaty on arms limitation had just been signed. The leadership in advocating this measure was pacifying the conservatives who felt that SALT-1 might endanger American security. On the other hand, they antagonized the liberals who applauded the agreement and wanted the arms race to slow down. The argument used to win over the latter was that the Soviets visibly intended to develop their armament within the agreed limits and the United States should not be overtaken; they must acquire more bargaining power for future negotiations: new programs would give them precisely that. The Soviets probably reacted in the same way as they made rapid advances in developing MIRVs.

A year later, the results of SALT-1 were not conclusive. Yet for the first time the two powers had succeeded in curbing their armament effort in some areas and in making firm and stringent arrangements in extremely complex matters. To evaluate its importance, the new relation has to be compared with the previous situation when there was no communication on strategic questions and be seen in the light of an increasingly complex international scene conditioned by the nuclear factor. From then on the new problem had to be faced squarely.

The most promising sign of change in this respect was the start of an on-going process. The SALT negotiations created a climate in which military détente could influence relations between the two parties and even the two blocs: the day before SALT-1 was signed an agreement for the prevention of incidents on the seas and in the air space above was concluded; one month earlier, on April 10, 1972, the two teams had signed a convention ruling out research, production and stockpiling of chemical or bacteriological weapons and prescribing their destruction. In May 1972, Brezhnev agreed to enter into preliminary negotiations on mutual reduction of forces in Europe, which led a few months later, in Vienna, to the start of the MBFR (mutual and balanced reduction of forces) multilateral talks between NATO and the Warsaw Pact. Moreover, between 1973 and 1975, under the auspices of the CSCE, the two blocs negotiated measures intended to restore relations of trust between East and West (e.g., all maneuvers involving more than 25,000 men had to be announced beforehand, etc.). Finally, negotiations did not end with the conclusion of SALT-1. The two countries seemed to favor a slow and gradual policy of arms control which would introduce a series of partial measures covering increasingly varied areas, and might in time bring about a balance in strategic forces.

The SALT-1 agreements seemed to be significant insofar as they were not isolated. The fact that they were part of an overall policy made them meaningful. SALT-1 "did not stand on its own, an odd and isolated phenomenon, taking place in a climate of hostility, at all times exposed to a sudden crisis," as Kissinger pointed out in 1972. "Rather it was organically bound to a series of agreements and a wide consensus on the international behavior to adopt in order to face the dangers of the nuclear era."

There was real hope that the two opponents, through discussions, exchanges of information on doctrines and strategic programs, and agreements that might be reached, would manage to understand each other and arrive at nuclear balance, until progress achieved in this field could be brought to bear on other sectors.

4

DÉTENTE: TRADE BENEFITS

"Economic relations exert an influence stronger than the intentions or decisions of any government and enemy class: they force them to get in touch with us." Lenin did not only point out the political benefit to be gained from foreign trade, he put the idea into practice. His successors followed the same policy, at one time or another, as they saw fit. Leonid Brezhnev and Alexei Kosygin did not depart from this tradition: they were convinced that such commercial platforms were best for détente; if they developed commercial exchanges with the United States, they would gain technological know-how and obtain the support of American business circles. For the last twenty years, a rigid body of regulations, established in the US immediately after the Second World War to prevent any risk of helping Soviet potential along, had kept commercial relations between the two countries to a minimum. Khrushchev had made every effort to convince the Americans to do away with this system, but had failed. His successors were luckier and, in a few months, relations became normalized.

TRADE AND COLD WAR

After World War II, as East-West political relations worsened, economic links were severed between the Unites States and USSR and two separate economic entities were constituted. The USSR withdrew within itself and the socialist camp: Stalin's post-war economic policy was characterized by the creation and consolidation of this "new world market" together with maximum economic independence in relation with the non-communist world. The monopoly exercised by government on external trade enabled it to control all exchanges with foreign countries, so that the USSR did not need special regulations to alter the course of its economic policy. This was not the case in the United States where foreign trade, considered as a sector in which, in principle, the government should not intervene, was by and large left to private initiative. Thus the latter could only influence exchanges with the Soviet bloc if it controlled them.

This is what happened in the late 1940s: from then on trade with the USSR was not conducted according to private economic interests (as it was in the inter-war period), but national security. In February 1949, the authorities started to control exports in general under the

49

new Export Control Act. The law aimed at "protecting the national economy in the event of shortages," and also and above all "supporting foreign policy and protecting national security." Control was exercised through a system of permits: export of all sensitive products required a valid permit (itemized and detailed). To start with, the government sought to limit export of material capable of contributing to the growth of military potential in the Soviet bloc. In 1962, the 1949 law was amended in order to affect not only the military but also the economic potential of Warsaw Pact countries.

Imports were also controlled and limited, mainly by means of steep tariffs. In 1951, President Truman suspended all preferential treatment in import duties for communist countries (apart from Yugoslavia): this brought to an end the 1937 commercial agreement through which the USSR had the status of most-favored-nation (a clause enabling countries belonging to this category to pay lower commercial duties).

The United States also tried to coordinate export control measures with those taken by their allies concerning the countries of the Eastern bloc, so as to prevent the latter from obtaining material of strategic value. In November 1949, a Coordination Committee was set up to that end; it was made up of the United States and six European countries in the beginning, but later was enlarged to include all the members of NATO (except Iceland) with the addition of Japan. Its task was to coordinate export control measures concerning the East and to draw up detailed lists of strategic products, some of which being subjected to an embargo, while others came under close scrutiny.

As a consequence of these measures, and of the policy of economic self-sufficiency adopted by the USSR, in the climate of East-West antagonism, American exports to this part of the world fell sharply between 1950 and 1955 and imports dropped likewise.

By 1952 a change had already occurred in the situation and in the 1960s pressures for a reappraisal became irresistible and the US was in a quandary: the USSR looked for ways of developing commercial relations with Western industrial countries and the Europeans, like the Japanese, responded positively to these advances, seeing the need for less strict definitions of products to be called "strategic" or otherwise. Changes in their allies' attitude in these years made American controls largely ineffective. Yet the matter of trading with the USSR remained taboo until the late 1960s: in 1963-64, a deal was made involving a substantial amount of wheat to be sold to the latter, but it was a one-time operation. All draft laws put forward to increase exchanges were rejected. When the Nixon Administration took over, the US share of Western trade with the USSR and Eastern Europe was very small (about 3% for exports and 2% for imports); the regulations set up at the height of the Cold War remained largely in place. Yet many were heard within the ranks of Congress and of the Administration, as well as in business circles, protesting this policy.

A NEW APPROACH

At the time the Soviets expressed a strong wish to develop commercial relations with the United States; they pointed out the many potential benefits to both sides which would arise from them. They still refused to admit that it was a necessity for them, since the USSR was supposed to have everything it needed for economic growth. Yet self-sufficiency was not a rational economic policy to adopt. The country had been forced, because of Western antagonism, to keep commercial links at a level much lower than it would have wished. The USSR wished to widen the scope of economic relations and make full use of the advantages of the international division of labor. One could detect behind these arguments a reappraisal of the part to be played by foreign trade in the country's economy as the Soviet leaders chose to get outside assistance to remedy internal shortcomings, and a belief that trade had a political role in détente: it represented the "material basis" which supported and strengthened relations between the two countries. To the Soviets, economic and commercial cooperation with the United States was an essential element of détente.

Since the Soviet government had a monopoly, the redirection of foreign trade could be effected at the stroke of a pen; there might be economic or political obstacles, but no legislative amendments were called for. In the Unites States a more complicated process was necessary and new laws had to be passed.

The problem of trade with the East had arisen already by 1969: in June of that year, the 1949 Export Control Act was due to expire, so it was a matter either of re-enacting the law or having a different one. President Nixon favored the former solution for a two-year period. The House of Representatives approved this decision but the Senate voted against it. Senators Mondale and Muskie put forward an Export Promotion Act which would have done away with the old control policy. A heated debate took place. Those who favored liberalization argued that Cold War antagonism had died down and the Soviets obtained every technical assistance from the Europeans and the Japanese; re-enacting the 1949 law was economically harmful to the United States (American export dealers were debarred from East European markets) and served no political purpose. They did not require an end to export controls, but proposed that the government should follow more or less the same policy as the Europeans and Japanese, that is to say using economic criteria in decision-making for non-military goods and radically dissociating commercial and politic relations. Some senators opposed this notion: they were convinced that the pursuit of commercial advantages was a short-term goal which put national security at risk and instead they called for trade to remain conditioned by political imperatives.

The government was also divided. The president refused to liberalize legislation without political gain, since he believed that an increase in commercial exchanges would not improve political relations, but rather the opposite. The Defense Department was the only supporter of this point of view. The Department of State and the Trade Department stood unreservedly for normalization; the former expected the political atmosphere to benefit from it, the latter, finding itself under pressure from business circles, saw no difference between what was good for the country and what was good for the economy.

Finally Congress passed a law drafted in more moderate terms than those advocated by Senators Mondale and Muskie, but altered the 1949 Act drastically and went a long way towards liberalization. Under the 1969 Export Administration Act, which replaced the 1949 Export Control Act, the United States declared itself in favor of "peaceful trade" with the East. Protecting national security remained the primary aim of the new regulation: exports had to be controlled whenever security was involved and the definition of such controls as well as their enforcement had to be agreed with the United States' allies; the president was empowered to rule out all exports to a nation which presented a threat to the American national security, without reference to other criteria. Yet economic considerations such as availability of goods abroad, consequences for the balance of payments—that is to say, factors conducive to commercial growth— were also taken into account in framing a new policy. The law, recognizing that unjustified restrictions could harm the United States, made provisions for an amendment to the list of controlled products which would answer such concerns. Moreover, the needs of national security were pegged only to those exports capable of strengthening the military capability of the receiving country. Also, an ambiguous and ill-defined link with economic potential (a 1962 addition to the 1949 Act) no longer existed.

The 1969 Act did not wipe out the old control policy: its wording remained very cautious and the application was left largely in the hands of the president. But a new approach could be detected which allowed trade with Eastern European countries to become freer. In the years following, export controls were greatly reduced especially as regards the number of products unilaterally controlled by the United States.

However, in practice, the situation did not change significantly until 1972 because the White House refused to normalize relations as long as political conditions had not improved. It resisted pressures brought to bear on decision-makers as control lists became shorter and economic difficulties (inflation, a weak dollar, balance of payments deficits—$9.8 billion in 1970; 29.7 and 10.1 in 1971 and 1972) made relaxation more urgent. Throughout 1971, little enthusiasm was shown and negotiations were interrupted or resumed following Soviet political moves. Proposals on the Kama lorry plant (KamAZ) were accepted after being held up for two years because the compromise on the SALT agreements had been successful and the Berlin settlement made a number of decisions possible; conversely, negotiations slowed down at the time of the India-Pakistan crisis. On June 11, another step forward was taken when dealers involved in the sale of cereals to the USSR and China were no longer required to produce individual permits for which detailed accounts had to be submitted. Since the abrogation of a clause which made it compulsory for 50% of American cereals sold to the USSR to be transported in US ships, the country was in a better position to trade with the Soviet Union; the 8 year-old regulation had made American wheat non-competitive on the market because of high shipping costs. As early as November, the USSR bought some 3 million tons of animal feed from the United States.

In the same year, Congress showed more flexibility in dealing with credit: it lifted the total ban affecting Eximbank (Export-Import Bank) since 1968, which prevented credit being granted to any country selling military or other kinds of material to a nation involved in armed conflict with the United States—the ban only applied to countries which were themselves at war with the United

States—and restored to the president the right to decide whether it was in the nation's interest for the Eximbank to guarantee, insure or grant credit to a communist country.

About the same time, the Trade Secretary, M. Stans, officially declared that economic interests should not be sacrificed to political considerations. His trip to Moscow in November comforted him in this assumption; trade was desirable in and of itself because mutual benefit ensued; it must not become a pawn on the diplomatic board. In December 1971, P.G. Peterson, Assistant to the President for Economic International Affairs, also declared himself in favor of a change of attitude towards the communist countries so as to improve the United States' economic prospects and ease the way of the Eastern bloc into the international community.

All the same, the White House maintained that no serious decision should be made while political problems were still unresolved. When Kissinger stayed in Moscow in April 1972 to pave the way for the presidential visit, he avoided all economic discussions, in spite of Brezhnev's attempts to engage him on this subject. At the summit, no important commercial negotiation took place, although the Soviet leader had half-jokingly declared to Nixon that USSR-US relations would make rapid progress if the latter granted $3 or 4 billion in credit spread over 25 years at a rate of 2%. Yet a joint Trade Commission, chaired by the American Trade Secretary and the Soviet Minister for Foreign Trade was established in order to negotiate a commercial agreement. After the meeting, Nixon eased regulations and progress was soon made: on July 8, 1972, he announced that an important agreement was to be concluded regarding agriculture, and on October 18 of the same year, a commercial agreement was signed providing a solution to many problems.

In August, P.G. Peterson, then Trade Secretary, declared himself strongly in favor of developing trade with the USSR. In his opinion, in an era of nuclear parity, security could not be achieved by arms only. Commercial relations both followed and influenced the political climate. Only an improvement in political relations could help an increase in economic relations, but once economic links had been established, common interests thus created encouraged progress in political relations.

AGREEMENT ON GRAIN TRADE

The agricultural agreement of July 8, 1972, was a landmark in the history of trade between the two countries, not only because it paved the way for a huge transaction, but above all because for the first time it was not a one-shot operation (as in 1963-64).

Under this agreement, the USSR was to buy $750 million worth of American grain over the next three years (August 1, 1972 to July 31, 1975), and the United States granted a corresponding amount of credit through the CCC (Commodity Credit Corp.) at 6-1/8 interest rate, which were normal conditions in those days. (During the Secretary of Agriculture's trip to the Soviet Union in April 1972, the same conditions had been rejected and the Soviet leaders declared themselves interested in credit at a rate of about 2% over ten years). It was clear from the conditions of this agreement that the two countries tacitly recognized common interests. They had come a long way since 1964, when any long-term transaction would have appeared as a favor to the Soviet Union.

Soon the benefits of such cooperation, dimly perceived in 1971, became increasingly obvious. In 1972, the Soviet crop, after a harsh winter and a short summer, had been a catastrophe. The Soviet leaders, forced to buy abroad, were relieved to find resources available in the United States: they purchased about 25% of the overall crop of American wheat in 1972 (11.3 million tons) as well as 6.2 million tons of maize and 1 million tons of soya. Total Soviet grain imports amounted to 19 million tons. The USSR had never made such enormous purchases, which markedly distorted the American market. These transactions, though they did not take place under the best circumstances for the United States, were useful all the same. They made it possible to absorb huge surpluses, whose stockpiling was expensive and unnecessary (Congress and the General Accounting Office were particularly keen to sell), and they helped to raise the price of agricultural produce which had stagnated for ten years, much to the government's concern. The deal was also welcome financially since the balance of payments' deficit had reached record levels.

Three years later, on October 20, 1975, the parties committed themselves further through a five-year agreement intended to regulate and stabilize exchanges. The Soviets promised to buy at least 6 million tons of American grain yearly; they would be able to buy two million tons extra if the American harvest was plentiful (above

225 million metric tons); beyond this amount, the agreement laid conditions for consultations between the two governments.

The USSR experienced wide variations in harvest levels from one year to the next: 181.2 million metric tons in 1971; 168.2 in 1972; 222.5 in 1973; 195.7 in 1974; 140.1 in 1975 (Soviet figures). Moreover its production costs were high, much higher than in the United States. B. Kerblay worked out that "a ton of wheat or butter bought from the US costs only half what it costs to produce it in the USSR; as for corn, soya, eggs, meat, American prices amount on average to a quarter of the cost in the Soviet Union." Obviously the two countries complemented each other. The new element was that the government faced the situation squarely and was willing to turn to the United States for help on a large scale and over a long period. The agreement of October 20 enabled the USSR to make up for bad harvests (for instance in 1975 hardly two-thirds of the objectives outlined in the Plan were fulfilled), to create stocks in good years and thus to stabilize the level of food for human consumption and cattle feed—in short, to face the hazards of production without making the consumer suffer from the consequences. The sale of grain was in the interest of the United States as surpluses were commercialized and prices kept at a decent level, provided sales were well regulated: the agreement of October 20, following the June 19, 1973, agreement, answered this concern. Prospects were thus hopeful in this sector with both parties keen to achieve regular co-operation in order to benefit from complementary needs.

OVERALL SETTLEMENT OF URGENT PROBLEMS

The trade agreement followed shortly after the May 1972 summit and was finally signed in Washington, on October 18, 1972, when the Trade Commission was in session for the second time. P.G. Peterson, the American Trade Secretary, and N.S. Patolichev, Soviet Minister for Foreign Trade, put their names to it and it was valid for three years. In addition, an agreement was concluded on the settlement of war debts, a declaration of President Nixon authorized the Eximbank to grant credit to the USSR and a maritime agreement was signed.

Trade agreements had already been signed in 1935 and 1937. However, the 1972 one went much further. It was an attempt to give a legal framework to bilateral trade and to regulate commercial exchanges between a planned economy and a market one. President

Nixon wanted it to cover all main aspects of trade between the two countries, to solve the basic problems which had long plagued their relations so as to allow for mutually advantageous commercial relations capable of development and finding solutions to any further difficulties that might arise. His ambition was to create a framework for American private enterprises in which to trade with the USSR. The agreement made allowances for specific problems of exchanges between a market economy and one in which the state enjoyed a monopoly in foreign trade; it granted guarantees to the United States against any mishaps that might occur due to imports being under exclusive state control in the USSR, as well as in exports and prices, which were not always linked with costs. The United States could take adequate measures to prevent Soviet exports causing full-scale or partial disruption in the American domestic market due to bulk or conditions of sale. As for the Soviet Union, it promised not to export to the United States goods listed by the American government as capable of upsetting the market. A consultation procedure was established to settle any difficulties which might arise.

Under the terms of this agreement, the United States undertook to grant the USSR the status of most-favored-nation. It was the only point that needed approval by Congress: the agreement was not put into practice until the latter had given its assent. Other measures were to facilitate the growth of trade. The agreement allowed for a trade bureau to be set up in Moscow by the American government, as part of its Embassy, while the Soviet government would have an office for trade in Washington. The members of these two organizations were to enjoy special privileges and diplomatic immunity. Moreover, the USSR would be able to open offices to conduct important deals, like the one involving the Kama lorry plant and American firms could have business premises in the USSR. Only two of them had such facilities in Moscow at the time. The Soviets were now willing to recognize henceforth such enterprises "which were known world-wide and had demonstrated their capacity to become commercial partners of Soviet foreign trade organizations with which they had entered into substantial trade contracts," and promised to allow accredited American firms to employ Soviet personnel, to acquire or import the necessary equipment (telephones, telex, typewriters, automobiles) and to have access to housing. Concerning disputes, the agreement advocated settlement through a third country acting as arbiter: up until then, except if it had been spelled out in the contract, the Soviets resorted to an arbitration commission made up of Soviet citizens.

Under these circumstances, the two governments expected overall bilateral trade to rise three-fold in the three following years compared to the period 1969-71; this was a minimum which, in P.G. Peterson's estimation, would certainly be exceeded.

On October 18, apart from the trade agreement, both parties succeeded, 27 years after World War II had ended, in reaching an understanding on the settlement of war debts. This problem had long been unresolved, remaining a subject of litigation which cast a shadow on relations between the two countries and slowed down expansion in trade. The 1934 Johnson Act made it impossible, in principle, to extend credit for more than six months (and in reality, impossible over the long term) to a country owing a debt to the American government.

Goods delivered under the Lease-Lend arrangement amounted to $11 billion. Out of this sum, the United States did not ask to be paid either for military material, or for equipment destroyed in the war, but only for civilian supplies that was stockpiled in the USSR on the day of Japan's surrender. Negotiations on this question started in 1947 but got bogged down by 1951, as the USSR refused to pay more than $300 million and the United States insisted on $800 million at least. On October 18, 1972, both countries agreed on a sum of $722 million to be paid by the USSR. The first three payments were agreed on: $12 million on October 18, 1972; $24 million on July 1, 1973; and $12 million on July 1, 1975. The remainder, that is to say $674 million, had to be paid in regular installments of equal value spread over 25 to 30 years, from the day the USSR received the status of most-favored-nation (a condition drafted into the agreement as the Soviets requested). The whole amount had to be cleared by July 1, 2001. This agreement, which ended a prolonged legal dispute, was inspired by the British settlement. It represented a balanced compromise, in the words of the Trade Secretary, in view of the historical importance and the emotional content of the question.

A maritime agreement, signed on October 14, 1972, complemented these negotiations. It guaranteed to the merchant navy of each country the right to transport a third of the goods exchanged, the remaining third being allocated to foreign ships. Forty ports in each country would, from then on, be open to commercial ships of the other fleet on condition of four days' notice being given (previously it had been 14 days). The agreement, valid for three years, included a proviso: Soviet ships used for transport to Cuba, North Vietnam and North Korea could not benefit from supply facilities in American ports, nor take on board goods whose transport was subsidized by the American government.

The Nixon Administration was satisfied that all outstanding serious problems between the two countries had been taken care of; most of them were of long duration, and the fact that they had found a solution indicated that an important step had been taken on the way to normalizing relations. The Trade Commission whose task was to oversee the agreement's implementation would be able to smooth over any difficulty that might arise. An Economic and Trade Council, a joint body set up in September 1973, was intended to assist businessmen and encourage commercial exchanges.

At the time Congress was in favor of this development. In 1971, it extended the validity of the 1969 Act until May 1972, and in the following year, continued to relax controls after a debate (less heated than in 1969) had taken place over the economic damage suffered by the United States as a result of strict trade limitation. Amendments to the 1969 Act that were passed focused on two points, the first being changes in control lists so as to do away with unilateral export control on goods available in other countries, except in cases which might endanger national security. The second point was coordination between the government and business circles: the law required the government to consult qualified individuals before granting or refusing an export permit—Technical Advisory Committees made up of industrial experts and government representatives were to be set up to answer this need. Further amendments were passed in 1974 to make it easier for American businessmen to obtain permits (administrative services were to reply to applications within 90 days) so as not to be at a disadvantage. Further, the protection of national security was to be improved: the Defense Secretary would have increased power.

The concept of trade with the East had changed significantly in the United States. Since the end of the war, the political line regarding trade had been one of sanctions and limitations with occasional relaxation. It was regarded now more and more from the point of view of profit to be made by both sides. Trade with these countries also acquired the stamp of respectability which it had lacked so far. An opinion poll carried out in the mid-1970s was quite clear on this point: 96% of the companies concerned supported détente with the

USSR; 86% judged Soviet-American trade to be beneficial to the American economy and 81% believed that increasing trade would improve the chances for world peace. Many of them did not understand why the government detected a threat to national security in the matter. About 70% thought that export limitations undermined the competitiveness of American firms, and 56% had no qualms about selling to the Soviet Union their most modern techniques. And 61% considered there was less danger in getting raw material from the USSR than from the Middle East, for example. A large proportion of the companies answering the questionnaire feared the emergence of the Soviet Union as a rival for the West, thanks to technological transfer, but 82% still declared themselves in favor of growth in commercial exchanges.

Trade being thus supported by business circles, by Congress (since 1969) and from 1972 by the White House, changes were to be expected. The first results of this new attitude did indeed look promising.

FIRST RESULTS

After the 1972 summit a number of ventures were in the works—these were the days when you could not open *The Wall Street Journal* or *The Financial Times* without reading about a new one—and important contracts were signed. The USSR received its first loan from the Eximbank in February 1973 and more in the following months ($469 million altogether). A. Hammer, the man who had known Lenin and his entourage well in the days following the Soviet Revolution and was now head of Occidental Petroleum, engaged in huge deals. On April 12, 1973, he signed a contract through which the USSR, over twenty years, would supply to the United States ammonia, urea and potassium, in exchange for the US shipping 4 fertilizer plants to the USSR and delivering enriched sulfurous acid. This deal was an example to follow, in the opinion of Soviet leaders. On September 18 of the same year, Hammer signed another one, which had been announced in 1972 and concerned a huge International Commercial Complex to be built in Moscow, with offices, hotel, and apartments for representatives of foreign companies living in the capital, lecture rooms, etc. One year earlier, on July 19, 1972, he had signed a five-year agreement for cooperation with the State Committee for Science and Techniques. Hammer and Occidental Petroleum were not alone in taking advantage of the new market. Pepsi-Cola concluded a contract for building a factory in the USSR: the American company supplied the technology and was paid in vodka; it also became the exclusive agent for the sale of all Soviet wines in the United States. Several American firms shared in building the gigantic Kama lorry plant (these lorries would be sent to Afghanistan a few years later). Agreements concerning the plant were signed in 1972 with a branch of Pullman, Swindell Dressler (for delivery of material and technical know-how for smelting works).

Among the plans under discussion, the most important dealt with the exploitation of Siberian oil, the United States being paid in kind for technical expertise and credit. This idea was taken up a few years later by the Europeans and attracted much criticism from the Americans. Yet the latter, in the early 1970s, seriously examined three projects. One was to do with Yakutia with the Americans prospecting and laying a pipe-line, with possible Japanese participation, which would go from Yakutsk to Nakhodka near Vladivostok and building a plant for turning gas into liquid form in Nakhodka.

By 1972, with some of these projects realized and the sales of grain, the volume of trade between the two countries had increased sharply. Sales of grain constituted the bulk of the rise; they made up from 45 to 75% of Soviet imports from the United States annually between 1972 and 1979. In 1970 and 1971, the United States was only in the ninth position among Western business partners of the USSR; in 1972, the US came sixth, and in 1973, second.

The first consequences of détente in trade were therefore on the whole economically positive. Sustained and imaginative efforts made by the two countries to overcome obstacles and provide a framework for cooperation had paid off. They encouraged a multitude of projects for cooperation and an increase in the volume of exchanges. This trend was to continue and become more significant as it offered many economic advantages. The USSR and the United States were the most powerful economies in the world and they both enjoyed vast natural resources, though not of the same nature. Although their structures were incompatible (labor, capital, etc.), both achieved good results in different fields. They proved to be natural trade partners, as Trade Secretary Peterson showed in his August 1972 report. Thus the future seemed promising in this area which provided a material base for détente, together with scientific and technical cooperation.

5

DÉTENTE: EXCHANGE OF TECHNOLOGY, IDEAS AND MEN

"We have to take all the good things from foreign countries: Soviet power plus American technique...equals socialism," so said Lenin in the early days and his successors fully endorsed his opinion: Although scientific and technical cooperation with the United States was largely responsible for the first attempts at industrialization made in the Soviet Union, after the Second World War relations fell to an all-time low, together with trade, and have played a negligible part in Soviet-American dealings since then. On January 27, 1958, an agreement valid for two years was reached in the field of scientific, technical, cultural and related exchanges, to be renewed later, but, between 1958 and 1971, it amounted to visits of information only; contacts remained extremely limited due to tensions between the two countries. Conversely, from the early 1960s, the USSR established strong links with European countries in this area: agreements for scientific and technical exchanges were signed with France in 1966 and 1971, with Italy in 1966, with Great Britain in 1968, and with Sweden in 1970.

BRIDGE-BUILDING

After 1970, a thaw in political relations made it possible to encourage growing cooperation in many areas, with the two governments actively participating. Technical exchanges were a convenient means for providing détente with a solid basis, laying a network of connections between the two countries. The USSR was very much in favor of such development: the United States with its size and resources was a more adequate partner than the European countries. Cooperation would be in keeping with Lenin's wishes and with the help of the more advanced American techniques, the Soviet Union would take great strides in various fields. Khrushchev's ambition was to catch up with the United States. His successors wanted to emulate advances made in the United States with its assistance, hence the Soviet intention to establish a network of well-structured and diversified relations on a much wider scale than with other western countries.

On April 11, 1972, a new agreement on exchanges and cooperation in the field of science, technique, education, and culture (to replace the 1958 one) called for an increase in cooperation. Under the same framework, it was followed by other agreements on specific areas which had, for the most part, been concluded at the end of the first three summits. Nine of them gave rise to joint commissions whose task was to supervise the implementation of the treaties and to encourage cooperation; the latter became institutionalized. The part they were meant to play was spelled out in the document "Fundamental Principles": they were to afford stability in exchanges and to give permanence to ventures that would be launched. They had two chairmen, one American and the other Soviet, both occupying positions of responsibility in government, and meeting at least once a year in plenary session, alternately in each country; in between sessions, they delegated their powers to two executive bodies—one for each side—whose members kept in touch, informing each other of their achievements, coordinating the various branches of the enterprise, providing a channel of communication between researchers and government departments, and controlling the work done. In the United States, the secretaries of these executive bodies met monthly as a committee which kept in direct contact with the National Security Council. Due to the overall view it gained from the arrangement, the NSC was able to direct the operations.

This institutionalized cooperation was given such structures to answer the need for consolidating détente, thus helping to reduce tension and improve relations between the two countries. The mechanism to promote a better understanding was outlined in the wording of the agreements to be signed as well as in various declarations. By setting up a network of strong and fruitful exchanges which linked individuals and institutions, the new approach was intended to bring together two widely differing societies, and make them realize that their interests lay in cooperation rather than confrontation, to encourage détente and create a feeling of mutual dependency—it would not wipe out the possibility of a conflict, but make it less likely. It was hoped that an increase in contacts between leaders and various personalities would improve understanding and lead to a gradual breaking down of the barriers that separated the two countries. Putting their relations on a sounder basis, it would make them more stable and help to create conditions more favorable to a dispassionate appraisal of problems. The momentum acquired by the new policy would make it irreversible. The political angle thus given to cooperation was encapsulated in the wording of the agreements: on the whole, they used general terms not intended to answer specific requests made by specialists; above all, they were signed by government members, some of them by Richard Nixon and Leonid Brezhnev or Alexei Kosygin in person, a political seal acting as guarantee for realization. In the scientific field, as in trade or strategic weapons, political will was needed to put cooperation on track. After the latter had been launched, exchanges would add substance to the new relationship.

Though the two sides agreed on the advisability of bridge-building, they did not view it in the same light. The Americans had a political objective in mind: they wanted to put into effect the policy backed by President Johnson on May 23, 1964. The Soviet objective was different: it put first and foremost the scientific and technical advantages to be gained from a policy of collaboration. From the start, there was a risk of imbalance in the enterprise: the Soviets might draw a major benefit from American technological advances without bringing a comparable advantage to the other side, and they could use it directly or indirectly to further military purposes. In order to prevent this, the American government required cooperation to be based on reciprocal advantages and above all to respect each country's legislation, that is to say, that all technological transfers be referred to American export controls (the two points were spelled out in the text of the agreements). To limit the extent of the damage, because the Soviet Union usually found it difficult to apply technological advances to industry, exchanges were directed towards fundamental research rather than business technology. The working of the agreements was closely monitored through the NSC by way of the committee of secretaries of the executive bodies.

TECHNOLOGY AND SCIENCE AS HANDMAIDS TO DÉTENTE

The combination of scientific and technical interests with political will was bound to result in fruitful cooperation. The first figures were indeed promising. In the four years following the May 1972 summit, the agreements brought forth some 150 programs of cooperation.

The agreements reached obeyed the same imperative: to join forces so that the experience and potential of each side, even their equipment, would contribute to the advancement of science and techniques. A wide spectrum of areas was covered, but three of them stood out: one because it was the finest expression of the new policy due to its spectacular character—that is, space research; the other two because the interests of both countries were widely differing but complementary: agriculture and energy.

The most global of these agreements was one on cooperation in the field of science and technology, signed in Moscow on May 24, 1972, by Secretary of State Rogers, and the Chairman of the State Committee for Science and Technology, V. Kirillin; the two parties undertook to encourage and develop cooperation through exchanges of scientists and specialists, exchange of information, joint planning and realization of research programs. As early as July 1972, M.E. David, scientific adviser to President Nixon, together with the Soviet team, outlined the areas to be given precedence: energy, agriculture, chemical research, water resources, protein production and computer use. These areas were further delineated by the Joint Commission when it met in Moscow in March 1973.

From then on cooperation made rapid progress. Under the terms of this first agreement, some 150 scientists and experts exchanged visits. In the five years following the signing of the agreement, twelve research teams were appointed. Towards the end of 1975, out of 49 projects approved, 26 were under way. The most efficient research teams, from the American point of view, were those dealing with electrometallurgy (research on electrical fields to protect ingots, welding with plasma, extraction and reduction of metals, welding materials capable of withstanding pressure, etc.) and chemical catalysis (organic metals used as catalysts, detailed studies of selected catalyst systems and of life supports for catalysts, environment control with special reference to decomposition of nitric acid, etc.). As for the Soviets, they were delighted with a number of projects, especially those concerned with the use of computers in management.

Many agreements for cooperation with American companies were signed at the time. In 1976, the USSR State Committee for Science and Techniques concluded fifty-three such agreements: 9 in the field of radio, television and electronics, 6 in engineering, 5 in the treatment of information, 5 in air navigation, 4 in machine tools, 4 in machines for foodstuffs, and so forth. The American firms involved in agreements were mostly large companies: Arthur Andersen, Boeing Co., Coca-Cola, Dresser Industries, General Electric, Gulf Oil, Hewlett-Packard, International Harvester, ITT Corporation, and Occidental Petroleum. Many of them followed commercial motivations: these agreements offered a way of penetrating the Soviet market.

There is a sector in which relations with the Soviets did not threaten to degenerate into technological transfers that might be used for military purposes, even in an indirect manner, namely, the health sector. This area of science had long been one of fruitful exchanges for the two countries, on a modest but steady scale, and had not suffered much from the climate of Cold War.

In 1970, the United States suggested active cooperation with the Soviets. This proposal was accepted in January 1971, and on May 23, 1972, a treaty of cooperation in matters of medical research and public health was signed. According to the American Secretary for Health, this agreement would allow two scientifically advanced communities to push forward the frontiers of knowledge, to save time and money, and to afford better opportunities for scientific breakthroughs. The two sides chose to focus their attention on cardiovascular illnesses and cancer, where cooperation would find an expression in joint scientific research projects, in conferences and gatherings of specialists, exchange of information, equipment, pharmaceutical products and technological methods, meetings for training medical personnel in the use of new apparatuses and equipment, etc. The agreement made provisions for joint funding by the health ministry of each country, an arrangement not reached in other sectors.

In the months that followed, cooperation got off to a good start and by the third summit a second agreement for cooperation in the field of artificial heart research was added to the one signed on May 23. Late in 1975, out of 30 projects approved, 19 were under way. They soon proved beneficial to both parties. Joint experimentation with new medicines and treatments for heart attacks and arteriosclerosis and chemotherapy for cancer made it possible to multiply data in a minimum time with a much smaller work team, and to improve on the reliability of results at little extra cost.

The peaceful use of nuclear energy, on the other hand, was an area where many possibilities for cooperation existed, but which would be kept out of bounds because of its military implications. Yet it was the subject of a cooperation agreement. In November 1970, the two sides decided to join forces to do research with the help of the Serpukhov and Batavia accelerators. On September 28, 1972, the Soviet State Committee for the Use of Nuclear Energy and the American Commission for Nuclear Energy agreed on a memorandum of cooperation and one year later, on June 21, 1973, the efforts made by each party brought about an agreement valid for two years (most of the agreements were for five years) on cooperation. It was signed by Brezhnev and Nixon and outlined three main areas: controlled thermonuclear fission, fast colliding neutron regenerative reactors, and the study of the fundamental properties of matter. Another area of study was defined in December 1975: light water reactors.

In the following months, information was exchanged and visits were planned. For example, under the auspices of the program of research into fundamental properties of matter, in 1975 two American scientists spent five months at Dubna, and another scientist one month at Serpukhov, while six Soviet scientists stayed at Batavia to carry out joint experiments with their American colleagues on antineutrinos with material that was in part Soviet.

Other agreements were signed; one of them on environmental protection (May 23, 1972) seemed to reflect serious concern in the USSR: the latter expressed satisfaction with the results obtained under the terms of the document outlining eleven sectors for cooperation. The balance sheet, according to the American chairman of the Joint Commission, soon proved positive: the work accomplished thus far made it possible to forecast earthquakes more accurately.

Another treaty dealt with oceanic research (June 19, 1973) giving it a formal basis and widening the field of research carried out by scientists in each country previously. This was an area which soon proved promising. Late in 1975, 15 research programs were under way (such as investigation into the interaction between atmosphere and ocean, sea currents and forces, marine geology, etc.). A third treaty concerned transport (June 19, 1973). It concentrated on technology for bridge and tunnel building as well as air travel safety and future forms of transport. A fourth treaty was to do with construction (June 28, 1974). Initially it dealt with questions of safety, resistance to wear and quality, building techniques in regions affected by earthquakes and in difficult climatic conditions (cold or arid). Three more agreements were mentioned earlier.

SPACE MISSION

In 1959, when Nixon visited the USSR, he suggested in a televised speech that American and Soviet personnel should go together to the moon. Little did he suspect then that he was instigating a spectacular and momentous joint mission into space which would be launched a few years later. Such collaboration would have been unthinkable in another period and caused a stir because of the popular appeal of the programs, while heralding the end of a particular phase of the Cold War as well as a pause in the costly rivalry between the two countries in their conquest of space. The rivalry had started in 1957 when the Soviets launched their first sputnik.

By 1970, the two countries had already built a basis for cooperation: bilateral agreements on space research were signed in June 1962 and in November 1965, as well a treaty in January 1967 on the principles which would guide the activities of signatory countries in the field of exploration and use of the atmosphere. Yet they never went beyond the stage of exchanging information. In 1970, for the first time negotiations started on two technical agreements which were concluded by NASA and the USSR Academy of Science: one, on January 21, 1971 and the other, on April 6, 1972, concerning an operation of docking by American and Soviet spaceships in orbit round the earth. The two agreements were included in one signed on May 24, 1972, by Nixon and Kosygin, which concerned cooperation in the field of exploration and use of cosmic space for peaceful purposes. The two parties undertook to carry them out and 1975 was the time chosen for the first experimental flight including junction in space of the spaceships Soyuz and Apollo with an exchange of passengers from one to the other ship.

The 1970-71 negotiations were the start of fruitful cooperation between the two countries: exchange of samples taken from the moon's surface, studies on space biology (experiments on animals' reaction in space, on the effect of weightlessness on the life of red corpuscles, on the hormonal contents of the pituitary gland, and on the growth of bone tissue, etc.), on the exploration of planets (information supplied by the USSR to the United States after probes had been sent to Venus, exchange of information on Mars that had been gathered by the American Mariner-9 device and the Mars-2 and -3 Soviet probes, etc.). Thus cooperation went much further than the more spectacular objective of a docking operation.

The preparation of this mission required frequent visits on each side. The Soviet crew stayed at Houston, at the plant where Apollo was built, Rockwell International in California, and at Cape Canaveral. American engineers and technicians, for the first time, were allowed to visit the base at Tyuratam and the space center at

Baykonur in Kazakhstan (the first Soviet space center); up until then, only de Gaulle and Pompidou had been invited to visit it.

The success of the operation, coming at the end of three years of intensive efforts, demanded a solution to many problems arising from the docking of the space ships: a linking module was drawn by the two countries, later to be built by Rockwell International for NASA; the pressurization systems had to be harmonized and for this purpose the Soviets aligned themselves on the American methods; to be able to communicate, the American crew learnt to speak Russian and vice-versa. Simulation work bringing together air controllers took place at Houston and Moscow.

Finally all difficulties were overcome and the operation was a complete success. Having been planned several years in advance, it went ahead on schedule. On July 15, 1975, Soyuz 19 was launched from the Tyuratam site and about seven hours later, three American astronauts left Cape Canaveral aboard Apollo. They docked as planned, on an orbit straight above northeastern Spain and the crews spent 47 hours together, during which time they carried out several experiments, an artificial eclipse of the sun among them with Apollo obstructing the sun by placing itself between it and Soyuz so that the Soviets could take photographs of the sun's crown.

This operation which originally was planned to build a docking system suitable for transfer of crews and capable of being used again, was a scientific feat; in particular it was a first step towards rescue operations in space. Yet it was an achievement which had no immediate application. The Soviets turned down the American proposal for another joint flight in 1976; NASA used the Apollo cabin another time, but from then on it directed its efforts on a half-rocket half-airplane air shuttle, which went into space in the early 1980s; the docking module was never used again.

This does not mean that the operation ended in an impasse, only that it fulfilled political objectives as much as scientific ones. The cost of the operation was such ($250 million for the United States) that it could not have been approved by the American Congress for purely scientific purposes, as several missions to the moon had been canceled in the past owing to drastic cuts inflicted on the NASA budget. The joint flight allowed the two countries to become acquainted with each other's space programs and to influence public opinion in each country in a favorable way (the event having received large media coverage) as to the other's development. It gave a spectacular proof of the superpowers' ability to overcome their differences and draw a benefit from cooperation. This was the message expressed by Leonid Brezhnev on September 22, 1975, when he greeted the returning crews.

COMPLEMENTARY INTERESTS: AGRICULTURE AND ENERGY

The agreement signed on June 19, 1973, in Washington, by Gromyko and Butz on agriculture corresponded to very different concerns on the part of each country. It was an area in which the differences between the two countries was widest: in 1971 the USSR employed eight times more people in agriculture than did the United States, which had 60% more land under cultivation; in the USSR an agricultural worker supplied food for 7 persons, while he fed 46 in the United States. The United States had 5% of its labor force in agriculture, the USSR one third—a much higher proportion than any of the other industrial nations. In the United States, most of the growth in production was gained through increased productivity, which was far from being the case in the USSR. These widely differing results, in spite of the huge investments made by the Soviet government in this sector of the economy, were sufficient to explain the interest shown by the Soviets in cooperation between the two countries. The Americans had another kind of motivation: it was clearly to do with information and estimations for the future. The Soviet leaders, in the early 1970s, altered their trade policy in agricultural products, largely relying on the world market to make up yearly shortfalls in their grain production, so that by 1972 they had become net importers of cereals. At the time, they seriously unbalanced the American market through massive purchase of grain. This operation, involving direct deals with large American companies, without control from the American government, cost the Treasury several hundred million dollars in the form of subsidies (the low prices obtained at the time on the world market were compensated by government funding). It also started a rise in inflation, as increased demand pushed prices up. Obviously the Americans were keen to continue selling their surpluses of foodstuffs which were difficult to put into the commercial circuit, but only under the right conditions: to avoid more unregulated and unexpected buying, together with variations in prices, they had to be informed of the precise needs of the USSR so as to adjust supply.

It was no coincidence that the agreement of June 19 was signed a few months after the disaster mentioned above: it was meant to set into motion the mechanism of complementarity that would benefit both countries. It had two separate aspects: one was to do with advance information and the ability to plan by providing regular estimates of levels of production, consumption, demand and trade regarding the main sectors of agricultural produce, research into econometric methods of forecasting predictions of demand and consumption. The agreement outlined the need for the parties "to encourage as much as possible exchange visits by scientists and experts in the areas of their respective countries where these measures might be applied." The other part of the agreement concerned agriculture *per se*: cultivation of agricultural produce (genetics, selection and protection of vegetable species, cultivation of agricultural products in subtropical zones), cattle and poultry breeding, agronomy, mechanization in agriculture, use, preservation and transportation of mineral fertilizers and other chemical products, conditioning of agricultural produce (especially for animal feed), artificial fertilizing, and the use of mathematics and computers in agriculture.

The agreement took effect without delay. The commission met for the first time in November 1973, and from then on regularly towards the end of each year. As could be expected, the Soviets soon displayed much interest for the latter area of research as defined in the treaty, while they were much cooler regarding the former. By 1974, they had supplied eighteen series of data—some of which had to do with grain production—but they were not sufficient for the Americans to make accurate prediction of imports into the USSR. The joint commission approved a proposal from the Americans to exchange delegations for checking on crops; yet in August 1974, the Soviets refused to give the American envoys access to the main areas of grain production. The following year was more promising for the Americans, but they still could not visit all the regions concerned. Perhaps because of these difficulties, late in 1975, out of eight research projects, only two were producing results.

In the field of energy, the same problems arose. In the USSR as much as in the United States, energy was a matter of urgency: although the USSR was by then the first oil producer in the world, a net exporter and had huge reserves in all sectors, the pace of growth of its production had slowed down since 1955 and the ratio of reserves to production was falling, with production ever increasing but no new oil-field of any size having been discovered since the early 1960s. Many regions seemed potentially rich (such as Eastern

Siberia, Sea of Barentz, Sea of Kara, Sea of Okhotsk, and the Arctic regions) but prospecting was kept at a minimum and most were located in difficult terrain, hence the willingness of the Soviets to cooperate with the Americans, the latter being in many ways ahead from the technological point of view.

The United States were interested in certain Soviet techniques such as magneto-hydro-dynamics: the Soviets disposed of the largest such generator in the world, while the Americans only had small experimental apparatuses. However, what they were after in reality was to gain a better insight into the energy policy adopted by the USSR and its appraisal of its rank in the world energy market. This concern became more acute after the 1973 oil crisis. An energy crisis in the Soviet Union would cause serious strains in the East— the USSR exported large quantities of oil to Eastern Europe (Bulgaria, GDR, Hungary)—as well as to the West, since the presence of the USSR and, in its wake, of Eastern European countries on the world market would disorganize it fatally. This fact led the United States to a realization that it was perhaps necessary for them to help the USSR to solve its energy problems through cooperation in the exploitation of Siberian resources. Besides, it would allow Western countries to diversify their sources of supply, thus reducing dangerous dependence on a small number of producers.

An agreement was signed on June 28, 1974, in Moscow, which responded to these various considerations. Two main objectives were set: first, widening the scope of cooperation to search and prospect existing fields of energy as well as new ones to replace those, finding ways of avoiding waste in transportation and use; and second, inducing better understanding of the other country's short and long term programs in this area. Under the terms of the convention, cooperation would bear on "technology relating to prospecting, extraction, treatment and use of organic fuel, that is to say petroleum oil, shale oil, natural gas and coal among others (in particular the new methods for drilling and accelerating the rate of production and extraction of oil and gas)"; "the exchange of information, of opinion and forecast concerning national energy programs"; "the technology for developing new sources of energy." Like the agreement on agriculture, it made provisions for exchange visits by researchers and experts to the regions of interest for the realization of the planned measures. The joint commission met in October 1974 and teams of scientists got down to work over the next few months, initially on a project concerning magneto-hydro-dynamics.

The implementation of all these agreements was attentively followed on each side. Everyone knew that potentially they were very significant, yet the Soviets showed themselves much more optimistic than the Americans regarding results. The surveys carried out in the United States from 1974 to 1976 stated that they had been very satisfactory, in some cases, but generally limited in their scope, and that more meetings and discussions took place than successful research work. Very often the blame for delays in establishing real cooperation, very necessary by common account, was laid at the door of the bureaucratic and political hurdles set up by the Soviets. From this point of view the situation was even worse in cultural matters.

CULTURAL LINKS

The overall agreement on contacts, exchanges and cooperation signed on June 19, 1973, in Washington by Andrei Gromyko and William Rogers, show that the United States and the USSR were equally keen to normalize relations in the area of culture. The agreement which emphasized their wish to encourage and develop contacts and cooperation, even in sectors which were not specifically mentioned in the document, listed a remarkable number of possibilities. The two parties promised to facilitate exchanges in education and research (students, teachers, researchers, teaching material for schools and higher education, books, journals, newspapers), as well as in the arts (theater, music and dance companies, orchestras and other art organizations, soloists, playwrights, museum directors, exhibitions, films, radio and television programs), in politics (deputies to the Supreme Soviet, American Congressmen, representatives of urban and regional authorities), and in social work (youth movements, women's associations) and to allow all the persons or groupings which were interested in certain questions to get information. They also undertook to encourage the study of each other's language and to open their doors to tourism which would enable interested people "to become familiar with the daily life, work conditions and culture of each country."

Such an agreement offered nothing surprising on the American side, but it expressed an attitude of good will quite novel on the Soviet side; if taken literally, it announced unprecedented transparency, only limited by the regulations of Article 18: the size of delegations, the program and all details concerning exchanges and tours had to be settled at least 30 days beforehand.

In reality, in spite of the agreement, it was clear from the beginning—and this would be confirmed later—that the two countries did not expect anything spectacular in the way of détente from this quarter. The Soviets did not count on new relations being established at this level. They fully intended to be far from open in this area. They wanted to exchange ideas and personnel to do with science and techniques; their interest obviously lay in this direction but the phenomenon would have to be contained so as to avoid political risks. Building bridges between societies would allow dangerous comparisons and eventually the regime might have to become more flexible. As will be seen later, the Soviet government had not the least intention of encouraging this trend: it was not interested in relaxing its grip. The way the Soviet leaders directed the operation proved that, to their mind, there was no question of tolerating free relations: for example, they insisted on their right to appoint the Soviet scientists who would take part in research programs in the United States, rather than accepting the choice made by the Americans on their list of invitations. This was an important sign: the authorities' ability to select the persons visiting the United States meant they kept a tight rein on cooperation.

Under the circumstances it is not surprising that cultural relations got off to a slow start. In education and research, a survey made in 1974 revealed that the United States and the USSR had exchanged, so far, some 200 researchers only; out of those, less than 10 taught or lectured and less than 100 remained longer than a semester. This turn-out does not seem to have increased much in the following years in spite of the start in 1971 of an informal program of contacts with a number of institutes affiliated to the Academy of Science of the USSR, the setting up of a Joint Commission on Social Sciences in 1974, and, in 1976, an agreement for cooperation between the Lemonosov University of Moscow and the State University of Moscow. Cooperation also soon proved unbalanced, because most of the Americans taking part in the exchange programs were linguists, historians or specialists in literature, while a large majority of the Soviet delegates were scientists or technicians. The USSR tried in fact, as far as possible, to take advantage of cultural relations to develop scientific connections. In the arts, exchanges were mostly isolated events such as tours made by ballet companies and orchestras, or exhibitions of paintings. As for the economic sector, realizations failed to match the promises of 1973: there was a huge gap between the number of Americans going to the USSR and Soviet experts staying in the US (91,800 against 16,000 in 1977 according to Soviet sources) and the American share in tourism remained smaller than that of other western countries which were physically closer but much smaller, such as West Germany or Finland (116,000 Germans and 949,000 Finns traveled to the USSR in 1977). As the Americans found out when they drew the final figures for cultural exchanges, these were disappointing.

Whether in the political, economic, scientific and technical, or strategic field, the efforts made by the leaders of each country were enormous. In many areas channels were established, sustained cooperation developed, and a variety of structures allowed for the needs of each party to be taken into account. Thus détente acquired some substance over the years. None of the agreements taken on its own was determining. No particular sector of collaboration was by itself sufficient to exert a long term influence on relations. Yet the process of drawing agreements, entering into negotiations, launching joint enterprises significantly altered relations between the countries. Never before, since 1917, was such an attempt made. Never was such a number of bridges built. Never did the superpowers try to give coexistence such a positive aspect. What were their objectives?

6

DÉTENTE: WHAT DID THE SUPERPOWERS WANT?

Slowly but surely the superpowers established a new relationship. What was the hidden motive for this difficult enterprise? Did it merely express a desire to reap the benefit of cooperation and to show good-will? Did it reveal a common purpose? Each country's leaders had their own notion of détente, their own reasons for applying this policy, their own objectives. Yet, as their declarations demonstrate clearly, they shared the same ambition and joined forces to put it into effect.

ESTABLISHING A DIALOGUE

What the superpowers wished more than anything else was to improve communication between them and put it on a regular and positive basis. In so doing, the leaders of the two countries drew inspiration from two new principles: they were conscious of being equal and of deriving a mutual advantage from cooperation. The right to be different became recognized by the USSR. Many times in the past, but in vain, the latter had declared that dissimilarities regarding ideology and the social system did not constitute an obstacle to normal relations; now the United States admitted this in the "Fundamental Principles of their Relations," and also, more significantly, in dealing with their opposite number. In the same way, equality between the parties was recognized formally and in practice. The "Fundamental Principles" stated that it was the basic principle of their relations and the security of each; SALT-1 gave a framework to parity; the economic, scientific and technical agreements were based on the idea that the two countries would benefit equally from cooperation. As we shall see, there was a slight difference between the Soviet position on these two points (they had been advocating them for a long time), and that of the Americans, which was much less clear. But whatever reservations Washington may have entertained at the outset, the relations that followed were those of equal partners and each benefited from the new climate. The many agreements that were signed testified to a desire on each side to make use of cooperation and widen the scope of joint endeavors. It was an entirely new departure from the previous situation.

This new relationship did not affect the respective nations, only the state apparatuses. The Soviets did not have any intention of allowing the privileged relations existing between the two countries to apply to society itself, a point which the Americans respected implicitly for reasons which were made clear in 1973-74. Contrary to what happened in the United States, there was no popular debate on détente in the USSR. Concerning strategic questions, for example, throughout the negotiations the Soviet press was content to release information on the comings and goings of negotiators; after the agreements were signed, the text was published, but with no accompanying commentary to allow the man in the street to understand and evaluate the terms. As H. Smith, at the time correspondent of *The New York Times* in Moscow, pointed out, the Soviet people was not given the means to appreciate the kind of achievement the agreements represented. On the human level, as was mentioned above, contacts in scientific and cultural matters were, on the Soviet side, highly controlled and organized, to fit in with political considerations. It was not by chance that cultural exchanges did not reach the same level as trade relations. What was essential in the eyes of the leaders of each country, for different reasons, was to establish interstate links.

STABILIZING RELATIONS AND THE INTERNATIONAL BALANCE OF POWER

After a dialogue had been established, the two countries hoped to be able to put relations on an even keel, stressing privileged cooperation rather than confrontation. As the superpowers emphasized over and over again, they wished to make the process irreversible. In a communiqué released at the end of the Vladivostok discussions, that is to say when détente was already seriously threatened, the two parties stated their intention to "develop and make irreversible the process of improving" their relations. They wanted to put an end to recurring the cycles of hope and disappointment which had affected their dealings since 1933, and bind the "other" to cooperation. The material basis of détente (agreements, contracts, commissions, etc.), in giving substance to the new relationship, would strengthen the balance and lessen the risk of the first political crisis putting it in jeopardy.

The primary objective was to prevent nuclear war and limit as much as possible the risk of its erupting, whether by accident or not.

It was an ever-present preoccupation in the minds of the leaders of each state, as can be seen from the September 30, 1971, agreement with the decision to modernize the red telephone line, the May 25, 1972, document on the prevention of incidents in the high seas, or that of June 1973. The determination to control the awesome armaments that had been acquired answered the same purpose: SALT-1 was the first result of the new attitude.

The superpowers had no intention of stopping there. Their real ambition was to put the international situation on a stable basis. They wanted to contribute to a relaxation of world tension, so that regional conflicts (such as those in Vietnam or in the Middle East) did not degenerate and bring about a situation which would implicate them both directly, making the risk of war between them considerable. It was not enough to settle conflicts or disputes that might put them in opposition; they also had to prevent such situations as might make relations between them worse and help to find a solution to international problems in which they would become involved, even indirectly. They both recognized at this stage the need to exercise "restraint" (the Russian word *sderjannost* appeared several times in the Soviet texts) and not to try to derive unilateral advantages either directly or indirectly.

The superpowers realized that in this capacity special world responsibilities were invested in them. The USSR and the United States had to build a framework for peace, as Richard Nixon explained on May 19 before leaving for Moscow, in which:

> the two great nations will use their influence not only in dealing one with the other, but also in other parts of the world where they have special interests, in lessening the danger of aggression and encouraging the forces of peace.... There cannot be a peaceful international order without a constructive relationship between the United States and the USSR. There will be no international stability if the two countries do not adopt an attitude of restraint and do not use their enormous power to the service of mankind.

This idea was expressed again in the "Fundamental Principles." The wording of this document, if taken literally went very far: the aim of the two countries, as it appears there, was to act in such a way that a form of permanent peace was established throughout the world. The spelling out in black and white of a code of conduct was a symbol of their determination to establish standards and put their relationship on a smoother course. Henry Kissinger emphasized this point in his *Memoirs* (M.B., pp. 1306-1307, 1310): "These principles [...] aimed at laying down a pattern of behavior enabling us to assess whether real progress had been accomplished and in the name of which we could expose any infringement."

One year later, Leonid Brezhnev, in the United States, insisted on the responsibility of the superpowers in a speech for American television:

> From the climate of relations between our two countries depends in a large measure the general world climate. Neither economic power, nor military power, nor international prestige bestow on our countries additional rights; on the contrary, they impose on them special responsibilities respecting world peace, the prevention of war. The Soviet Union is fully conscious of this in its relations and dealings with the United States.

CREATING MECHANISMS FOR CONSULTATION

In order to play a responsible part in preserving the international balance of power, the superpowers had to enter consultations. The understanding they had of their commitments and duty to consult with each other was all important as it affected the international situation.

The two countries were fully conscious of the power they derived from their special relations. We know, Leonid Brezhnev is supposed to have said on the occasion of the second summit, that as regards influence and power, there are only two nations in the world which carry any weight, the Soviet Union and the United States: "Whatever we may decide between us, all the other nations will have to accept, even though they may disagree." We are not very far from the notion dear to Franklin D. Roosevelt who in his days had imagined for the three Great Powers—the United States, USSR, Great Britain (later to be joined by China)—the role of joint world policemen so as to preserve peace, by force if necessary. Did the United States and the USSR, in the early 1970s, try to play this part?

In the agreement on the prevention of nuclear war there was a clear attempt on the part of the two countries at setting up a system to defuse crises. There the superpowers showed themselves determined, just as in the "Fundamental Principles" to establish a mechanism for consultation which would prevent any situation arising capable of threatening détente either directly or indirectly. They went even further. Any conflicts that might degenerate into nuclear conflicts, in which they would have to act as arbiters, were circumscribed, so that in the end there were few crisis situations which remained outside their range. The agreement instituted new regulations for the conduct of international relations, according to which the two Great Powers would play the part of mediators, or even arbiters, in any quarrel that was likely to worsen. After the agreement was signed, this change of attitude in their international behavior raised strong suspicion, since some of the United States' allies (France especially) were afraid that consultation might lead to a condominium. To calm these fears, the latter did their utmost to play down the consequences of the treaty, and gave assurances that the allies had no cause to worry about the validity of their own agreements with the United States. Yet the enthusiasm with which the new dispositions were greeted in the Soviet Union was disquieting!

The San Clemente talks on the Middle East afford an insight as to the meaning of dialogue for each side: it seems that there was no understanding between the superpowers as to their conception of international cooperation. The Soviet approach, as expressed in the talks, was to preserve international order, of course, but also that the world balance, if it needed restoring, could only be preserved by the two Powers. Any kind of settlement, if negotiated under American guarantee only, would never be worth anything from their point of view. They wanted to take part in solving all major conflicts and oblige the Americans to admit the usefulness and necessity of this involvement, to abandon therefore their systematic search for rolling back Soviet influence. The fact that Brezhnev, on the last evening of his stay at San Clemente, demanded an explanation on the Middle East, against all the rules of diplomacy and even politeness, indicates that the Soviet leaders attached great importance to the question of consultation, that they were uncertain of its value in the mind of the Americans and they wanted a firm commitment.

This episode was a landmark in the history of détente, because it ended in disappointment for the Soviets by revealing differences with the Americans on a sensitive subject. The latter were conscious that Brezhnev was trying to prevent Soviet prestige in the Arab world being undermined and American influence in the region gaining ground, but they thought that Moscow was asking for help in imposing peace conditions to suit Arab requirements. They may have been slightly mistaken in their appreciation of the debate. What the Soviet leaders were seeking was probably not so much a peace treaty based on Arab demands (which would have been be unrealistic, as they well knew), as one resulting from an agreement between the super-powers; they used the Middle East as an example to try to impose the idea of allocating zones of influence in the Third World, or in some areas of the Third World, which would give legitimacy to their presence in these parts. The Soviets had good reasons to feel uneasy at the American stand on this question. The United States had no intention of allowing a crisis to transform the dialogue with the Soviet Union into a parceling-out of spheres of influence. The Soviet leaders became aware of this by 1973-74: it was one of the thorny questions which thwarted the policy of détente.

It is not surprising that the superpowers did not agree on such a vital matter. They meant to establish links between the two countries and outlined a wide area of joint interests, but they remained in opposition.

7

THE AMERICAN POINT OF VIEW: FROM CONFRONTATION TO NEGOTIATION

When Richard Nixon started his term of office on January 20, 1969, his objective was to drop confrontation and start negotiating instead. He knew this was a ambitious plan but one not impossible to realize. During the three years that followed, that is to say for three fourths of his first term of office, he probably doubted the success of this enterprise. The Soviet leaders, in spite of encouragement from the American side, showed no sign of changing their ways. Confrontation did not appear to be a thing of the past.

Even before his rise to power, Nixon let the Soviets know of his intention to negotiate. On December 18, 1968, Henry Kissinger met Sedoc, an Embassy adviser, to express the President's desire for reconciliation which would become grounded in reality if the Soviet leaders showed good will in the sensitive areas of the world such as the Middle East and Vietnam. The answer delivered on January 2, 1969, gave ground for hope to the new Administration (Kissinger, M.B., p. 133): it praised Nixon's "realism" and chose to ignore his past attitude (an allusion to his reputation as anti-communist). It "recognized that a settlement of the Vietnam problem, a political solution to the Middle Eastern conflict and a 'realistic approach' of the European problems in general, particularly the German one, would improve relations." The first wave of optimism did not last long: the years 1969 and 1970, though many meetings took place, as Kissinger described in his *Memoirs*, were marked by confrontation, anxiety and inextricable situations.

Vietnam was, of course, the main hurdle. As soon as he took office, Nixon made it clear to the Soviet leaders that progress in any negotiation whatsoever would depend on their attitude on Vietnam, and that their reluctance to help the United States to bring the war to an end prevented the latter from having anything but formal relations with the USSR. Until 1972, the Soviets did not respond to these requests, but insisted that they enjoyed only limited influence over Hanoi and gave the US no encouragement in this regard. Since the Soviet Union was the main supplier of military hardware to North Vietnam, the Americans could not accept this excuse. The situation was extremely embarrassing for the United States who could not pretend to ignore the part played by the Soviets in the war. At the same time, they sincerely wished to improve relations with the USSR: they needed its assistance to find a way out of the conflict and a spectacular success in foreign policy to heal the trauma caused by the war.

Vietnam was not the only obstacle to a rapprochement between the superpowers. Other events in the Middle East, Chile, Cuba, and Asia appeared to the Americans (Kissinger, M.B., p. 617) as "the various facets of a global communist challenge," since "none could have taken place if it had not been started or encouraged by the Communists," thus creating a climate of sharp tensions between them. The importance attributed by the Nixon government to the East-West conflict made the situation worse, since it looked at all the crises arising in the world as expressions of a struggle between the USSR and the West. The Americans played down the influence of local factors and exaggerated the consequences of these events on East-West relations.

The Middle East remained explosive. The moves of the USSR in these parts, especially the support it gave to Egypt, seemed highly dangerous to the United States. On January 31, 1970, Kosygin wrote to President Nixon (*Memoirs*, p. 348-9) that if Israel "continued on its adventurous course...the USSR would be forced to make sure that the Arab states had enough means at their disposal" to enable them to stand up to their attacker. In the next few months, this warning was put into effect: large quantities of Soviet weapons were delivered to Egypt, including sophisticated anti-aircraft materiel, and a few thousand instructors were dispatched, which looked to the Americans as if the Soviet leaders, instead of putting pressure on Nasser to accept a compromise, encouraged him to fight on. In September of the same year, Washington was alarmed at the crisis erupting in Jordan, as it was convinced that the Soviets had encouraged the Syrians and these in turn had fueled Palestinian anger. "We could not allow, Nixon wrote in his Memoirs [pp. 352-4], Hussein to be toppled by a Soviet-inspired insurrection."

During the same year, 1970, Cuba was the backdrop to another confrontation, as the Americans accused the Soviets of planning to build a base for nuclear U-boats at Cienfuegos, contrary to the 1962 agreement. The Americans, already concerned after Castro's declaration of military cooperation with the USSR, at a time when the economic insertion of his country into the Soviet bloc was well under way, became anxious upon hearing of a meeting between the Defense ministers, A. Grechko and R. Castro, which was followed by a number of Soviet ships calling in Cuban ports. President Nixon lost no time in responding sharply and demanded assurances from the Soviets that they would respect the 1962 agreement. Was this activity on the part of the USSR an attempt to force a trial of strength in Cuba? American public opinion did not take it seriously and the government saw the affair as a probe to test the resistance of the adversary, a way of ascertaining whether the declarations of good-will made by Nixon reflected "hesitancy, weakness...or an earnest desire to negotiate."

At the time these events took place, Salvador Allende was elected as president of Chile. This election introduced a socialist regime, in a legal and non-violent manner, into what the Americans considered as their sphere of influence, upsetting them deeply, especially since it coincided with two crises which looked to them as elements in the East-West conflict. They were convinced that this new development would inevitably inspire a communist expansion in the area, perhaps controlled by Moscow, and at the very least anti-American, so that the cohesion of their hemisphere would be threatened and, as a consequence, their national interests would come under attack. This was a decided setback for American influence from which communism benefited.

Late in 1971, nearly three years after Nixon had announced his intention to normalize relations, he was again faced with a crisis which, in his opinion, revealed the negative aspect of Soviet behavior. The war between India and Pakistan, starting on December 4, 1971, brought about increased tension due to the fact that the three Great Powers were involved with the protagonists. The USSR supported India and the treaty of friendship and cooperation signed on August 9, 1971, was a factor in the mounting hostility of India towards Pakistan, as the former received unconditional backing for its claims over its neighbor. The United States were bound to Pakistan by the Southeast Asia Pact of 1955, and by a treaty of mutual assistance signed in March 1959, a promise which was confirmed in November 1962. China was also heavily involved in Pakistan's fate. There was a danger of the conflict degenerating.

Throughout the crisis, the Americans put great pressure on the USSR to try to curb India's belligerence. On three occasions, Nixon wrote to Brezhnev and Kosygin to beg them to do their utmost to bring the crisis to an end; on December 12, he even made use of the "Red Line," which he had never done before. Kissinger warned Vorontsov, the Soviet chargé d'affaires in Washington—Dobrynin was away at the time—that the United States would fulfill their promises to Pakistan, they would not remain idle if China were threatened, and that an improvement in Soviet-American relations was not compatible with any Soviet support of a war in the Indian sub-continent. However justified the American concern, Moscow was not greatly impressed by it, since its position in the conflict was conditioned by considerations arising from its rivalry with China. In this context it was of great importance to win India's lasting gratitude and friendship, to give a solid basis to Soviet influence in a sensitive region through the establishment of strong links with Bangladesh, and to punish Pakistan for acting as an intermediary between China and the United States. Washington finally saw how things stood, and allowed rapprochement with Moscow, already well under way, to continue.

In spite of these crises, the normalization of the European situation lowered international tension and a risk of confrontation. Such normalization was made possible thanks to the American-Soviet first steps towards détente and, because it lessened the likelihood of a conflict, opened the way to better understanding between the superpowers. Due to Chancellor Brandt's Eastern policy and to Soviet goodwill, the status quo, as it was defined after the war, was confirmed by the USSR-BDR treaty signed in Moscow on August 12, 1970, which recognized the German partition, by the BDR-Poland treaty of December 7, 1970, and the Quadripartite agreement on Berlin of September 3, 1971. Berlin having been the theater of endless frictions and crises between the Great Powers since the war ended, the agreement by acknowledging the rights of the western powers in the city cleared the air and removed one of the main stumbling blocks in East-West relations. Détente rested mainly on a balance of forces: the latest agreements confirmed that such a balance existed in this part of the world and were therefore a major component of the structure.

THE BLOSSOMING OF DÉTENTE

Presidential reports on foreign policy drafted for the benefit of Congress are valuable witnesses to the changing perception of current events on the part of the government. The first one, published on February 18, 1970, stated that "relations with the USSR were on the whole still far from satisfactory"; in Vietnam, the Soviets bore a "heavy responsibility in the continuation of the war"; in the Middle East they were "neither realistic nor constructive...." One year later, on February 25, 1971, the President wrote in his report that, in spite of a few encouraging signs, "certain Soviet activities are, to our mind, of a disturbing nature."

The year 1971, according to the third report of February 9, 1972, was "the year of major changes." In that year, the United States had

> succeeded in giving a new impetus to the chances of more .
> positive relations through a series of concrete agreements
> bearing on sources of tension between the two countries. These
> agreements were of varying importance, yet they all provided
> serious reasons for believing that a fundamental improvement in
> American-Soviet relations was probably possible.

The report went on to list the treaty on denuclearization of the deep seas, the compromise on SALT-1 and 2, the approval given to a draft treaty banning production or possession of biological or toxic weapons, the agreement over Berlin, the measures to make the "Red Telephone Line" more efficient and others concerning the prevention of an accidental nuclear war, and the start of economic talks as encouraging developments. However, Nixon remained prudent, adding that although these measures might indicate the beginning of new relations with the USSR, other events (e.g., the development of Soviet armaments, deliveries of weapons to the Middle East, Soviet attitude during the India-Pakistan crisis, expansionist maritime policies, etc.) occurring in 1971, "do not give a clear indication whether we are witnessing at the moment a lasting evolution of Soviet policy or merely a short-term change induced by tactical considerations more than genuine commitment to a stable international system."

According to Kissinger, the US-China rapprochement was the key event which started things moving (M.B., p. 827-8, 894-5). After the announcement, on July 15, 1971, of his secret trip to Peking and of the presidential visit to the Peoples Republic of China, the Soviet leaders soon tried to improve relations with the United States and smooth the way in current negotiations (on Berlin and agreement on the accidental start of a nuclear war). As a matter of fact the talks on Berlin, during which the USSR made considerable concessions, came to a successful conclusion, late in August after 17 months of negotiations, and, on October 12, a joint declaration issued in Washington and Moscow confirmed that an official visit would be made by President Nixon to the USSR a few weeks after his return from China. Progress was made before July 15, 1971, regarding armaments: the compromise allowing negotiations to continue was reached in May. Yet in April, two developments, seemingly of little importance, but highly significant—an invitation to an American table tennis team to play in China, as announced on the 6th, and on the 14th, an American decision to bring the embargo on trade with China partially to an end—were evidence of the positive turn taken by China-US relations. On July 19, while the Soviets had thus far consistently dragged their feet, Dobrynin begged President Nixon to go to Moscow before his trip to China.

Similarly, the rapprochement between China and the US was perhaps the reason for the USSR seeking a confrontation in Asia a few weeks later. The India-Pakistan conflict enabled it to delineate the new balance between the three big powers, to show the United States that it would not hesitate in reacting sharply if the latter made too blatant use of the Chinese alliance and to expose China's incapacity to support its friends.

Finally the crises of 1970-71 made it possible for the USSR and the United States to test each other's reactions. In 1971, under the impact of the China-US rapprochement and the need for the Americans to extricate themselves from the Vietnamese quagmire, the two countries, in the atmosphere of détente prevailing after the recognition of a status quo in Europe, and following the 24th Congress of the CPSU, began to seek ways to normalize relations. However, it was not until May 1972 that Nixon considered he had reached his objective: Moscow, when faced with a choice between Washington and the North Vietnam ally, placed the United States first. Moscow thus jeopardized the "bonds of friendship, militant solidarity and brotherly cooperation" based on the principles of proletarian internationalism with the Democratic Republic of Vietnam which found itself isolated, in order to establish privileged links with the leading capitalist nation. Preference was given to negotiations with the United States rather than confrontation.

The talks "did not suddenly change an imperfect world into a perfect one" as President Nixon declared on his return from

Moscow, but there was a glimmer of hope that "the world would no longer live in the shadow of fear and war," and that "a process had started which might lead to lasting peace." The bases for new relations between the two most powerful countries in the world had been laid. He went on to say that, for the first time, real progress had been achieved in dealing with difficult questions, which have long obstructed the path of normal relations between the two countries:

> [The] trips to Moscow and Peking have started to free us from constant confrontation. We have moved towards a better understanding, mutual respect and point by point settlement of our differences.... We are advancing in the direction of a world in which the leaders of nations will settle their disputes through negotiation, not through force and in which they will learn to accept differences.

In Kissinger's opinion, the main achievement of this summit, besides some isolated results, was to "map out a framework for coexistence" with the USSR, and he thought the future very promising. Independent observers saw the summit in the same light: articles published in journals such as *Foreign Affairs* or *SSA*, which enable us to follow changing appreciations in one or the other country, were quite reserved before it took place; the emphasis was on the possibilities, potentialities and also uncertainties of Soviet-American relations. After the first meeting they became much more sanguine.

Then came the heyday of détente which Kissinger placed between 1972 and the second half of 1973 (Sakharov's letter to Congress and the October War—cf. *Disillusions*; M.B., p. 1311). It was a time when relations between the two countries were relaxed: they had never been so promising since the end of the Second World War. A number of links had been established, cooperation developed in all directions, a real exchange of views was made possible. In this period, the policy of détente seemed acceptable to the American people.

The superpowers acted with moderation in all international affairs. The Soviets trod cautiously in dealing with the Third World. In July 1972, the fact that they took calmly the decision of Sadat to expel their advisers from Egypt proves it: it was a logical conclusion to their disagreement which had been aggravated by the Soviet-American summit, during which the Egyptians thought that the USSR had not defended the case of its Arab allies with enough force. The peace agreement on Vietnam, reached on January 23, 1973, in

Paris (just after ex-President Johnson's death), however fragile, removed an obstacle to the development of relations between the two countries. In Europe also, a better balance seemed to be in the cards with the start of the Conference on Security and Cooperation in Helsinki in July, and in October in Vienna talks on the reduction of conventional forces. The MBFR (Mutual and Balanced Forces Reduction) from January 1973 were the subject of preliminary discussions. The CSCE had been at the top of Soviet preoccupations for twenty years and they attached much importance to its outcome. To the Americans it appeared as one element of the vast field of East-West negotiations, which might make relations in Europe more stable and smoother, as well as allowing free circulation of persons and ideas—in short, one more effort to move from confrontation to negotiation.

If the improvement in relations with Moscow was closely watched by some sectors of the American public which were more or less directly concerned, the man in the street followed it from a distance. He regarded the development which Nixon saw as a complete upheaval in the international balance with a certain amount of skepticism. The presidential trip to Peking aroused an enormous interest, but it was another matter for the Moscow visit. In 1972, what was uppermost in the mind of the average American was not Soviet-American relations, but the Vietnamese conflict. He fully approved the May 8 decision (maritime blockade of North Vietnam), without giving much thought to its possible consequences on the Moscow summit. When the latter took place, what he wanted to know above all else was whether decisions would be made concerning Vietnam. He approved of Nixon going to Moscow, saw the agreements that were signed as positive on the whole (while wondering what practical effect they would have), but in his opinion the summit would be a success only if the President obtained genuine Soviet help in bringing the conflict to an end.

In 1973, Brezhnev's visit to the United States did not arouse much interest either, much less than the one Khrushchev paid in 1959. By then public opinion was more concerned with the Watergate affair than with US-USSR relations, and the former was given more prominence than the latter in the press. Only when such a momentous event as the signing of the agreement on the prevention of nuclear war took place did relations with the Soviet Union take precedence in the media.

This lack of interest was even more striking in 1974. The third summit passed almost unnoticed: meetings with the Soviet leaders had become routine to the average American. What public opinion had been concerned about for some months was the problem of emigration, and in a wider context the question of human rights, which would later loom larger than any other.

This phenomenon of the man in the street showing little interest in superpower relations can be explained by the fact that the novelty had worn off (in contrast with Nixon's trip to China in 1972 or Khrushchev's to the United States in 1959), but also that the Soviet threat had lost much of its relevance. According to Gallup polls, the Americans had never been so favorably disposed towards the Soviet Union since World War II. Between 1954 and 1973, the proportion of people who thought well of the USSR increased from 5 to 34%, while those who disliked it went from 88 to 57%. The ones who thought ill of it fell from 75% in 1954 to 30% in 1973. In 1973, only 6% of the persons consulted (in May) considered the Soviet threat to be the most serious problem facing the United States at the time (*Herald Tribune*, June 20, 1973).

This does not mean that the Americans did not remain strongly anti-communist. Such an attitude was bred by some 25 years of Cold War. To use the expression describing the rivalry that opposed the two countries since the war, they did not think it possible to change Soviet mentality. Their president shared this opinion, but did not draw the same conclusions.

The man who had promised in the early days of his term of office to take the United States, after an era of confrontation, to the negotiating table and who succeeded in transforming the relations of his country with the Soviet Union and China, had a solid reputation, going back to the 1950s, for anti-communism, which is something of a paradox. As a matter of fact, the strong antagonism Nixon felt towards communism was not incompatible with the policy of détente that he devised with the assistance of his national security adviser, Kissinger, and his reputation was an asset in imposing it on the United States.

NO RECONCILIATION, ONLY COMMON INTERESTS

In a literal sense, détente meant relaxation of tensions. Nixon took it a step further. He was not content with avoiding conflicts, establishing tentative contacts, or mental attitudes. He conceived a full strategy, both firm and conciliatory, resorting to stick and carrot in turn, as he described it, which was intended to set up mechanisms for preserving peace over the long term, due to a balance of forces regarding strategic power as well as the position held by each of the superpowers worldwide. This strategy should, for the first time, enable the American government to lay the foundation for genuine coexistence with the USSR, and to change from turbulent relations to peaceful and stable ones.

The new policy was based on two principles: on the one hand, there were differences and antagonisms; on the other common interests were present. Both world powers continued to oppose each other. The American leaders being fully aware of the gap between themselves and the Soviets: they did not expect the latter to give up their basic aims and did not think that any conciliatory attitude they might adopt would result in a radical or partial change in Soviet hostility vis-à-vis the western countries. President Nixon wrote in his foreign policy report dated February 9, 1972:

> The problems dividing the United States and the USSR are serious and deep-seated. They are central to the system of security put into place by each country and to the balance between them. No mere improvement in the political climate can be expected to solve them, but concrete agreements on sensitive matters which are responsible for tension between our two countries. [...] Our differences are far-reaching; they are not due to temporary factors, nor to individual persons, nor to accidents of history. They are rooted in the history of each country. They are exacerbated by types of behavior which stem from our national characteristics and our differing approaches of the conduct of international affairs. We are ideological opponents and will remain so. We are in competition in the political and military field and neither of us can remain indifferent to any progress achieved by the other in this respect. We are both leaders of a group of countries; we both value our allies and are not willing to sacrifice them for the sake of improving relations. Each of us possesses an impressive nuclear capability, intended to counter the threat posed by the other's power. We both pursue global policies. If we are not careful of the actions we take, we can arouse fresh tension and be the source of conflicts. Our peoples are intensely conscious of half a century of active hostility. This historical fact is the mainspring of our efforts to bring in improved relations.

It is necessary to acknowledge differences of opinion. Richard Nixon wrote on February 25, 1971 (second report on foreign policy) "In our relations with the Soviets, we shall make more progress if we recognize that, in many cases, our national interests are not identical and it is useless to pretend otherwise; the points of disagreements arising between us are not to do with moods but are fundamental."

He repeated this theme on June 1, 1972, after his visit to Moscow: "Soviet ideology is in permanent opposition to some of the most basic American values and Soviet leaders are determined to uphold this ideology." However, even though "they are still and will remain in competition with us, [...] what we seek is to bring about a world in which we shall learn to live with differences of opinion, in which we can solve them through negotiation, not force."

American leaders, convinced that communist ideology was "the inspiration of Soviet foreign policy,...which turns interstate relations into conflicts between two philosophies," drew the conclusion that, in the minds of the Soviets, there was no scope for conciliation: any peace proposals on the part of the latter can only be due to a realization that the balance of forces is unfavorable to them. They decided to answer this problem with decisions based on the Soviet leaders' actions, not their declarations.

The policy of détente introduced by Nixon, as advocated by the new government on many occasions, did no entail any kind of reconciliation between the two countries' political systems, nor did it put an end to confrontation, or even tension. In this sense, it was a policy totally devoid of illusions.

Yet the realization of sustained competition between the two countries did not prevent American leaders from seeking an area of common interests, therefore possible cooperation. They meant to widen and strengthen this area as much as they could, so as to reduce the risk of conflicts and gradually change confrontation into partnership. To achieve this goal, they sought to enter negotiations in many sectors, to create an impetus which would spread in all directions and allow for progress all around—in short, benefit from its own dynamics. They wished to carry out negotiations within a strict framework, that is, on a reciprocal basis. This intention proved difficult to put into practice.

Détente, as Nixon defined it, appeared to be an attempt to find areas of concordance between the two countries. He wanted to establish a network of connections, to develop cooperation and exploit the Soviet desire to build bridges with the outside world. He tried to determine the boundaries to respect in a pattern of inherently competitive relations, to make the Soviet leaders aware of the advantages to be drawn from working hand-in-hand, and simultaneously, of the dangers of confrontation, thus introducing more moderation in their behavior. He did not see any way to bring about safer relations with the USSR other than by reconciling a competitive situation with the need for cooperation with an appeal to common interest and moderation. Increased cooperation would make it easier to "concentrate on contents rather than the atmosphere in which the deals were conducted" (February 9, 1972 report), to address problems dividing the two countries and find solutions.

A NEW POLICY FOR A NEW WORLD

A reformulation of relations with the USSR in the field of foreign policy was not merely a possibility. In the early 1970s, it had become necessary: the world had changed so much that the United States had to thoroughly reappraise its approach to foreign relations.

The map of the world had undergone radical alteration since World War II. The centers of power had become more numerous and their nature was not the same. The United States was no longer part of a bipolar world. It had ceased to be what it embodied immediately after the war: the only economic and military superpower, which was the reason why it had taken the responsibility of leader of the free world. The progress made by the Soviet Union had wiped out its strategic advantage. Western Europe and Japan had recovered their economic drive and political balance. China could no longer be ignored as a world power. New nations had made their appearance in the Third World. This development incited Nixon to ask from his partners inside the "free world" to reexamine their responsibilities and take up some of the burden (this became known as the Nixon Doctrine) so as to set up a new international structure based on negotiation and balance of forces rather than confrontation.

In this new approach the USSR played a major role. It represented at the time the most powerful nation-state in the world apart from the United States. Its military and naval potential, also to a slightly lesser degree its economic potential, and its participation in world affairs were growing. In the nuclear era, as Khrushchev had remarked in 1956, there was no alternative to peaceful coexistence, but since then, the balance of forces between the two world powers had become much more favorable to the USSR. While in the early 1960s at the time of the Cuban crisis, the United States enjoyed enormous strategic advantage (to the tune of 15 to 1 at the least, according to Nixon), early in the 1970s, the United States and the USSR were roughly equal (see Chapter 3). Ideological differences paled into insignificance in the face of the nuclear danger. The first priority was to avoid a nuclear conflict. On June 5, 1974, in Indianapolis, Nixon declared:

> We must never forget the harsh realities of the nuclear era. Since the USSR has reached parity with us regarding strategic weapons, each conflict has always implied a danger of nuclear devastation for all civilized nations. The lessening of tension between our two countries has become the top priority of our foreign policy. [...] The alternative to détente is a nuclear arms race which cannot be controlled, a return to constant confrontation and the collapse of our hopes of building a new structure for world peace.

The United States could not close its eyes to a power which grew "more vigorous, efficient and far-flung" (H. Sonnenfeldt). It was in its interest to exert some control over the rise of the USSR to the status of world power, and to make sure that such means it had acquired were used with moderation. The Nixon administration thought that this goal could be reached through détente.

The break-up of the communist bloc's unity was another vital factor in shaping changing international relations. New arrangements emerged which seemed hopeful to President Nixon. The bloc facing the United States became less of a threat and it was now possible to adopt a more flexible policy. The USSR had most to lose in the process: the break-up, forced on it by China, meant that there were two front lines instead of one. The situation was different for China, which found what it was seeking: freedom and autonomy. Nixon was convinced that the conflict, which came out in the open in 1963, and became exacerbated in 1969, opened up new vistas to the United States because it implied "a shift in energy and resources on to objectives other than a permanent challenge to the United States and their associates, and a higher priority granted [...] to the pursuit of national interests rather than subordinating these interests to the needs of world revolution." He pressed the two enemy-brothers to reassess their views on security.

The search for balance was not confined to the international stage: it concerned also the domestic front. The Vietnam war played havoc on the United States: it undermined the nation's self-confidence. In the puny southeast Asian country the American model had been rejected: the United States were obliged to use force to impose its political and social system and in the end it failed. The war was a terrible shock for the United States because it found it impossible to extricate itself from it: the US had no hope of winning, since it could not run the risk of escalation by using the means necessary for victory. At the same time, it could not afford to lose: disengagement must not turn into a rout, but a political settlement was difficult to achieve. In other words, the war aim was unrealistic and this basic flaw was responsible for the complete loss of morale among the military as well as ordinary citizens.

Nixon intended to pull his country out of its plight and give it new impetus. He wanted to find a new balance which would reflect the real world situation. He advocated following the course of realism rather than the old idealistic goals, and building a different world order, a structure to preserve peace which would rest on common interests. In order to succeed, he had to bring the Cold War to an end.

THE STRATEGY OF THE CARROT AND THE STICK

This was a realistic policy, adopted after many illusions had been wiped out (at least in the ideological field), and the necessity of negotiating with the opponent had become apparent in an age "colored by ideological differences and widely divergent views, but nevertheless when the two countries literally hold the survival of the human race in their hands" (H. Kissinger on May 29, 1972). Détente, in this setting, could not be merely a loosening of tension which would amount to the American opponent yielding some ground to Soviet claims for wider involvement in world affairs at the expense of the interests of the United States. This was not what Nixon had in mind, since he was deeply mistrustful and disapproving of the Soviet political system. Yet being pragmatic, he realized that circumstances forced him to use new methods while his objectives remained unchanged. What he wanted was to continue containment of the USSR. This task would no longer be achieved by isolation and resistance, but through a mixture of cooperation and resistance. By means of a subtle policy of rewards and sanctions, the carrot and stick approach, Nixon hoped not only to contain Soviet political advances, but also to guide them in a direction which would correspond to American interests, or at least cause minimum damage. Détente was thus not an alternative to the doctrine of containment, but an added feature. The strategy adopted by Nixon was remarkable in that it sought to make détente complement containment.

Détente was not a static notion; it was not a goal that could be said to have been achieved at any given time. It was a dynamic process, a type of relations aimed at giving the Soviets good reasons for cooperation with the United States, both encouraging them when they followed a policy which suited American interests and taking punitive measures if their policy went against American wishes. Intentions counted for nothing—only actions mattered, as well as willingness to implement agreements after they had been signed. The fact that any aggressive deed and attitude deemed irresponsible on the part of the Soviets brought about an immediate response from the Nixon administration was intended to steer the other side to the right course and keep it there. As for the Soviet leaders, they would obtain what they wanted, if in return they proved amenable to American desiderata.

Linking all problems together (the linkage system) was the underlying principle of this policy. The Johnson government had judged that each time a particular question seemed likely to find a solution, it was preferable to reach an agreement by keeping it separate, as far as possible, from possible repercussions on other conflicts. On the contrary, Nixon saw all basic problems as intimately linked, since the two countries' interests were far-flung and intertwined due to their being world powers. He did not think it advisable to have a conflictual situation in one sector and one of cooperation in another. This was the reason why Nixon made Soviet assistance in reaching a settlement over Vietnam a pre-condition to the establishment of normal relations. By spelling out to the adversary that he could not hope to benefit from confrontation *and* cooperation at any given time, that moreover all agreements must be made on a strictly reciprocal basis, the American leaders hoped to make the Soviets adopt a more moderate line.

The success of the enterprise depended in the end on the size of the "carrots," the trump cards available to the American government, and on their skill in making capital out of them during negotiations with the Moscow leaders. Trade, a sector in which

Nixon's advisers saw the Soviet side as being in an inferior position, is a good example of the role "carrots" were supposed to play. The government did not believe commercial links, on their own, however strong, would make the risk of war disappear, as political disputes were capable of overriding them. Yet they could serve as bait to the Soviets in return for political or diplomatic concessions, or inversely they could be cut in the event of conflicts and friction. They were useful as ways of applying pressure, encouraging cooperation, and granting rewards.

After an overall improvement in relations had been achieved due to the new tactics of encouragement and sanctions, the United States hoped to convince the USSR of the benefits of cooperation, benefits which would make the consequences of their disagreements appear as minimal; in other words, conditioning the USSR into thinking that it was in its interest to settle individual problems in a peaceful manner before they grew out of hand and to adapt its conduct to conform to American wishes so as to preserve cooperation and good relations. The USSR would find itself entangled in a web of agreements and ties so complicated that it would be impossible to sever them.

Kissinger declared on May 29, 1972: "We have tried to improve our relations on a wide spectrum of areas, as we thought that, on either side, this would create so many common interests on the edge of a more formal relationship that [...] it would result in a different attitude in conducting foreign affairs on both sides." Nixon hoped that concluding cooperation agreements "to turn cooperation into a matter of routine and strengthen institutional links" would incite the two parties to preserve good relations. Improvement in relations would provide "an encouragement for the two countries to minimize and contain the consequences of their disagreements, to persevere in the difficult process of negotiations and to avoid any deliberate return to hostility and confrontation." This dynamic process should become irreversible.

Nixon and Kissinger made every effort to get the USSR to adopt an attitude more respectful of American interests and show more moderation on the international scene. They tried to reduce the chances of direct confrontation between the two countries in areas of crisis, to enable each to control tensions at any time, to see the desirability of reaching a compromise rather than asserting their respective national interests. This strategy did not aim at altering the

Soviet internal system. The American leaders repeated on many occasions that they would shape their policy according to the actions of the USSR on the international stage and the way it would respect formal agreements, not according to its ideology or internal politics. They took the USSR as they found it—much to the Soviet leaders' delight—and asked for its cooperation while taking into account the variations in their interests. This concept of détente, which raised few eyebrows in the United States initially, became a subject of controversy from 1973 onwards, leading the government to explain its position more clearly. Kissinger went into it on March 7, 1974, while addressing the Senate's Financial Commission:

> Since détente is based on recognizing our differences and aimed at preventing disaster, there are limits to what we can ask for. [...] We may require from the USSR responsible behavior and therefore we did not hesitate in acting in a decisive manner during the Middle East crisis. We may also ask for formal agreements to be respected. But as for fundamental changes to the Soviet system, it is not a question of whether we are complacent in relation to Soviet internal affairs; it is knowing when and how far we may imperil other objectives (first and foremost the setting up of a peace structure) for the sake of these internal changes.

A few days later, President Nixon stressed the point:

> Our foreign policy must reflect our ideals and our intentions. By no means can we accept wiping out human liberties. [...] But there are limits to what we can do. [...] Not by choice, but in view of our capabilities, the guiding principle of our foreign policy must be to contribute in influencing the nations' international behavior on the world stage. We would not like other countries to intervene in our home affairs, and we cannot expect them to cooperate if we try to interfere in theirs. We cannot direct our foreign policy towards the transformation of other societies. In the nuclear era, our first responsibility must be the prevention of a war which could destroy all societies.

Richard Nixon's strategy is striking not only because of its coherence but also its complexity. Its application required two basic conditions: first of all, a large concentration of power in the hands of the President. As the strategy needed fine tuning and was conditioned by decisions which were not made in response to the technical factors relating to a particular problem, but to the degree of political maturation of the situation as a whole, it was imperative that all decisions rest with the same person and that their application be immune to any action a counter-power might take. With this in mind, Nixon decided, soon after he took office, to personally lead the negotiations with the USSR from the White House. It was to be expected that this assumption of the right to decide in a field as sensitive and important as relations with the USSR would not be easy to obtain in a democratic regime. This is exactly what happened. Once the negotiations had started, they acquired an impetus of their own, and various forces came into play. Thus, for example, according to Kissinger, pressures from Congress and the media left the president with no choice but to accept the start of the SALT talks without preliminary conditions, while in his first press conference, on January 27, 1969, Nixon had established a link between the SALT talks and the political situation. As time went on, the president found himself with less and less room for maneuver.

The other condition was for the United States to have the upper hand, including in the strategic field. The Nixon administration felt confident of having the means to influence the Soviets and to oppose any intention they might have of using détente as a cover to exacerbate local conflicts or to gain a predominant position in any part of the world or on a global scale. In order to achieve this aim and impress upon the USSR that aggression was not in its interest, the United States had to be strong and capable of enforcing its wishes— an approximate balance of power had to be preserved: two nations aware of their forces being approximately the same would think twice before attacking. This policy was not to be implemented by isolated shows of force, but it required a sustained effort to avoid showing weakness in any area whatsoever. The United States soon realized the difficulty of the enterprise, especially following a protracted and unpopular war, and at a time when the country's political life was undergoing a complete transformation. The US overestimated its ability to influence Soviet behavior and the significance of their assets and of the "carrots" at their disposal—this soon became clear.

When the Nixon government estimated that it was in a strong position in relation to the USSR, it was not only due to the resources of the US, but also to the international situation, namely the Chinese factor. Though it claimed not to exploit the Chinese-Soviet dispute, undoubtedly the success of its strategy, in the early months at least, depended largely on the possibilities this conflict offered. In the late

1960s, most American political scientists came to the conclusion that an improvement in relations with China would result in a chill with the USSR. Nixon, on the contrary, judged that by creating a new geopolitical balance between the three big powers he would be able to force a dialogue with the USSR. He was convinced that, as the Soviets were becoming obsessed by their quarrel with China, they would prove more flexible and conciliatory with the United States as they feared US rapprochement with China, a possibility which did not appear too remote in view of the convergence of interests between the two countries.

The American stance in the face of the two communist big powers was founded on unambiguous premises: in principle, they both represented a danger for the United States because of their aggressive ideology, in practice, the USSR's power and its actions on the international scene made the Soviet threat more of a danger than the Chinese one. It was not in the Americans' interest to let China draw near the USSR, nor allow the USSR to dominate or weaken China. In the event of a Soviet attack against China, the US would feel compelled to react; if the USSR annihilated China's military power, it would be tempted to go further so as to have a free hand in their struggle against the West. Thus, geopolitical realism and the international balance of power encouraged the United States to renew relations with China. As for the Chinese, they were keen to have a counterweight to their powerful neighbor. Soviet intervention in Czechoslovakia in 1968 and skirmishes on the Ossuri River in 1969 demonstrated that the Soviets would not hesitate to resort to military means to settle differences inside the communist world. The Soviets therefore represented a concrete threat to the Chinese, especially as since strong military pressure was exerted on their common border. During the 1960s, and above all after 1963 (with the treaty signed by Moscow concerning partial suspension of nuclear testing), China lost no opportunity in denouncing the USSR's betrayal in favor of the imperialist side and to protest her anti-imperialism, which gave her a chance to belittle the USSR among communist and Third World countries and to slow down, short of preventing, a rapprochement between the USSR and the United States. As China was uneasy about her powerful neighbor's intentions, she came to temper anti-imperialistic declarations and steer closer to the United States so as to counter the USSR and allow geopolitical factors concerning security more importance than ideological considerations.

Officially Nixon refused to point at either of the Chinese or the Soviets as the main opponent and, from the start, was careful to stress that the new relations with China were not "intended to affect any nation." Yet the Shanghai communiqué, signed at the close of President Nixon's visit to China, made it clear that the two countries had powerful common interests. It stressed that they did not wish to impose their hegemony in Asia and "would oppose any effort made by a country or an alliance to achieve such hegemony."

The United States, in taking advantage of the rivalry between China and the Soviet Union, had to tread warily; they had to be careful not to have the Chinese believe they represented only a temporary asset in the struggle with the USSR, to be discarded as soon as no longer needed. Mao made it clear that the US should not "climb on the back of the Chinese to reach Moscow." The United States was also mindful of getting too close to China and inciting the USSR to resort to desperate measures. The margin for maneuvering was extremely narrow. Apart from this reservation, the Nixon government was convinced that the opposition between China and the USSR would give it a chance to set up a new international arrangement.

In his search for détente, Nixon knew he had the support of his allies, a factor of great importance to him, since they were on close terms with the USSR and were keen for him to negotiate. Yet in this area also he had to be careful not to frighten his allies by his presentation of a realignment of the world map which, while giving them more autonomy and redefining their individual tasks, made them feel left out or exposed to new dangers. This is what mattered most to the Europeans: their main concern, in assessing the consequences of a China-USSR rapprochement, was the effect it would have on their security. They supported any move which might buttress it—this was the reason behind their efforts to have the Americans show more flexibility in dealing with Moscow—and worried about any development which might put it at risk. When the United States officially recognized parity and signed the June 1973 agreement, they thought the president had gone too far, fearing that they might suffer from too much relaxation of tension between the superpowers which could cause the United States to reduce it commitment in Europe. Nixon tried his best, with varying degrees of success, to soothe this anxiety. "We seek to establish better relations with our erstwhile opponents," but "we shall not abandon our friends and allies throughout the world. [...] Preserving the vitality, integrity and strength of our alliances in the free world is the basis on which all our other initiatives for world peace and security will rest," he declared on June 1, 1972, on his return from Moscow. His decision to make 1973 the "year of Europe" was his way of securing his allies' support. Such a move did not awaken much enthusiasm among Europeans, especially the French.

Richard Nixon did not have all the odds on his side when he stepped on the road to détente with the USSR, but he thought he had a good chance of success. He was convinced in any case that the only way for the United States to ensure peace and have its dynamism restored was through dialogue. The two parties would still be in opposition, but the benefits were obvious. The Soviet analysis was very similar.

8

DIALOGUE FROM
MOSCOW'S VIEWPOINT

The international status of the USSR became recognized after a series of long and patient efforts made by the leaders to establish a fruitful dialogue. Since Khrushchev's days, this aim was at the heart of Soviet foreign policy. In 1959, during his visit to the United States he had declared: "There cannot be peace and stability in the world so long as the two great powers are in opposition." Though these words had fallen on deaf ears, Khrushchev continued his campaign which was later taken up by his successors who wanted to spread the influence of the USSR worldwide and to reduce the gap separating it from the United States in the economic and, even more importantly, the strategic field. From the Soviet point of view, détente in the early 1970s was a follow-up to the peaceful coexistence advocated by Khrushchev in 1956: then, as in 1970, there was no valid alternative to this policy. The Americans took a long time to rally to these views, but at the start of the new decade, they came around: a visible change in their attitude toward the Soviet Union made it possible to establish a frank exchange of views based on a shared consciousness of power, sense of responsibility and appreciation of each other.

The USSR saw détente as a vital step in international relations. After the 1933 diplomatic recognition and the war-time alliance, this was the third stage of its relations with the most important world power and it appeared promising. It was also highly significant, since détente amounted to a de facto recognition that mattered more than the document signed in 1933. At the time, there had been some hope that the move meant the acceptance of the Soviet political system which would therefore result in good relations between the two nation-states. This obviously did not happen. The USSR remained despised, or at the very least ignored; in any case it was misunderstood by the leading world power, with no hope of belonging to the international community. The American attitude during and after the Second World War did not improve the situation.

Early in the 1970s, for the first time since the end of the war, the Soviets saw a real possibility for progress and hoped for a normalization of relations with the United States. The new factor was that the Americans had become more realistic at last and, sincerely this time, were ready to treat them as full members of the global community. During the war, President Roosevelt had acted along these lines, but only because he was forced to do so by the Nazi threat. As soon as that pressure had vanished, the United States went back to its superior attitude which, as Moscow knew full well, it had never been its intention to abandon over the long-term.

Now, on the contrary, the Americans accepted the USSR as it was and did not assume that they themselves were in a stronger position. It was a decisive moment in international relations and was based, as the Soviets saw it, on objective factors: the growing power of the USSR and of the entire socialist bloc, the balance of forces tilting to its advantage, the fact that there were less and less important problems capable of being solved without its agreement or without taking its interests into account. The American leaders, because of the USSR's power, were forced to be more realistic, to acknowledge the failure of their efforts to dominate world affairs, their failure to contain, annihilate or roll back socialism, to recognize the vitality of socialism and its ability to survive and, consequently, to accept a long period of coexistence between the two systems as inevitable. The new attitude of the United States made relaxation of tensions possible while strengthening peaceful coexistence between nation-states under different social systems.

Such a coexistence, in the Soviets' opinion, could only be beneficial. The United States acknowledged in the document on "Fundamental Principles" that equality and non-interference in internal affairs formed the basis of their relations from then on. This recognition, on which their new code of relations rested, represented an unprecedented victory for the USSR because it could be transposed in both political and moral terms. It appeared as the crowning of its new power and above all of its world position. The Soviet Union now was equal to the US and felt vindicated; the greatest world power had introduced it, as it were, into the international community so as to make it a partner of other western countries. Normalization of its international relations had been achieved.

This was a remarkable feat for a country whose very existence had been put into question by the United States, and which, among members of the international community, had long been treated as an outsider, almost an outcast, a country whose political system and behavior had attracted heavy criticism. Seeing now the most powerful nation in the world accept equality and responsibility in international affairs as the basis of their relations and a condition of global equilibrium was cause for rejoicing. Thus far, in practice, the position of the USSR had been recognized only in the socialist camp. Elsewhere, it was considered a revolutionary power almost and left in the shadows. It had been tolerated only because it was impossible to ignore it completely, although it was sometimes profitable to have commercial contacts with it.

Now it measured up to the United States as a superpower. The United States considered joint enterprises as possible and even advisable; it recognized that the two countries shared responsibilities in the global community. That was the crux of the matter. Since Soviet power was a political and strategic reality, the Americans would have been obliged to acknowledge it sooner or later. However, this factor did not oblige them to treat the USSR as a partner in world affairs. In so doing, the US indicated its esteem and granted the Soviets equality in the political as well as in the moral sense. They had won consideration following their accession to world power, which gave them enormous satisfaction.

A New Burst of Dynamism

The dialogue that Moscow worked so hard to establish was at the heart of a coherent and dynamic foreign policy which took shape in the late 1960s. After Khrushchev was dismissed, the new directorate found itself facing a situation in foreign affairs that was in many respects unsatisfactory. Khrushchev had succeeded in pulling his country's foreign policy out of the rigid and outdated framework left by Stalin and had given it a new impetus. This novel approach, beneficial for a time, had led to an impasse after a few years.

Regarding China, the Soviets had failed miserably. What could have become a formidable alliance between the two communist powers and would have resulted in setting up a vast communist bloc to oppose the West by reorganizing geopolitical forces on a global scale, had given rise to the emergence of a new rival which represented a considerable threat. China was a difficult neighbor for reasons of territory and strategy: disputes regarding Siberian tracts of land which the Chinese claimed as their own, demographic pressure exerted by China on the outskirts of the almost empty Siberian wastes, not to mention the presence of impressive conventional forces on the other side of an endless frontier. But above all, she represented a dangerous rival: although they inherited the same ideology, China was not content with refusing to obey or to act as younger brother to the oldest communist country. Instead she rejected the Soviet model as unorthodox, was forever critical of the USSR's decisions, and contested its right to act as leader of the other communist countries. Finally, she was zealous in seeking the support of Third World countries. She embodied an alternative socialist ideology whose economic concerns and the solutions offered were more suitable to developing countries than the ones advocated by the USSR, whose level of industrial development was higher. The communist movement refused to condemn her, in spite of repeated efforts made by the Soviet Union, as the 1969 conference made it clear.

In Africa Soviet influence had suffered a defeat after some brilliant successes (especially in Ghana and Mali). In the Middle East, the 1967 Arab defeat had demonstrated the Soviet failure to control the situation in the region.

After the Cuba crisis of 1962 and subsequent humiliating withdrawal, the USSR had felt cut off from the United States. There was no desire on the part of the Americans, apart from isolated instances, to draw closer to the Soviets; instead, they tried to apply the policy of bridge-building with the East European countries and met with some success in their efforts to undermine Soviet authority in the area by encouraging a spirit of independence.

The new Soviet leaders had no alternative but to face the fact of they were being driven into a defensive position; thus they needed a new policy to restore the balance. The 1968 crisis in Czechoslovakia marked a new departure: finding itself in a serious predicament—the Soviet-type political system was under attack—the leadership was compelled to brace itself for drastic action. The invasion of Czechoslovakia on August 21, 1968, proved to the socialist camp and the entire world that there were limits to be respected. Lack of response from Western countries showed that the Soviets had a free hand in a region which they considered as their sphere of influence and confirmed that Europe was split into two from ideological and political points of view. The action the USSR took had made its international position clear and indeed strengthened it. It could now claim that a socialist community did exist, one which would not disintegrate in the near future. The Soviet Union, as its main bulwark, could claim victory and, on the strength of it, embark on a new course in foreign policy.

This exercise proved positive for the USSR, but for a while it seemed highly dangerous. Many doubts were expressed by other communist countries on the validity and legitimacy of the Soviet-type political system. A short time later, in 1970, the Polish crisis confirmed the difficulties facing the socialist world. To overcome these problems, the Soviet leaders were obliged at all costs to restore their image inside the bloc and on the international stage. Establishing contacts with the West would benefit them both internally and externally. Such a move was a real necessity if they were to overcome the difficulties of the socialist camp in Europe, since remaining isolated would have been interpreted as a sign of weakness and the Western world would have been tempted to exploit the situation. In the end, the Soviet leaders were able make capital out of the crisis created by their intervention in Czechoslovakia, and used it as a stepping stone to clarify their position and move forward. During the following months, as they were confronted with a changing international situation—Germany's policy of opening up to the East, China-US rapprochement, China's admission to the United Nations—they adopted a new political stand which brought surprising results and changed their international posture.

CHINA-US RAPPROCHEMENT

Three main objectives were on the Soviet foreign policy agenda at the time: privileged relations with the United States, protection of the Eastern European preserve, and limitation of Chinese power. These objectives were interconnected: the empire in Eastern Europe was the cornerstone of Soviet influence. There was no ambiguity left in this area, so advances could now be made, within (by increasing integration) and without.

China represented the most pressing threat. The skirmishes which took place on the border in 1969 confirmed this fact. In assessing this risk, the USSR came to view the United States as central to international affairs. Military clashes were not likely to escalate because of the enormous capability of the Soviets, but they indicated strong hostility on the part of the Chinese: this factor had to be taken into account and would remain unchanged so long as Mao was at the helm. China itself, being weak, was no more than a potential threat, but could become a rival for influence inside the communist world and Third World countries, especially if she drew closer to the West and, above all, to the United States. As a matter of fact, since the end of the Cultural Revolution, the situation appeared more worrying: China was trying to come out of her isolation, to resume her role in the international community. She was admitted into the United Nations (in 1971), a forum she soon used to launch attacks on the USSR. More significantly, she was drawing closer to the United States: the announcement of President Nixon's visit to Peking, in February 1972, burst like a bomb in Moscow. An understanding between China and the US haunted the Soviet leaders: it would isolate them and upset the international balance. This catastrophe had to be avoided at all cost.

In the late 1960s, the USSR realized that China's progress on the international scene had to be curbed. A three-pronged strategy was adopted. First, it was necessary to contain China in the Third World, especially in Asia: Leonid Brezhnev's offer, in 1969, of a collective security pact was an attempt to circumscribe her, although the USSR protested that such was not its aim. The alliance with India was a first step in this direction. The second element was improving relations with China while keeping her under control. There were few chances of succeeding in dealing directly with the Chinese leadership, but tension could be lowered in some areas: in 1969 negotiations on border disputes and river traffic in sensitive areas were resumed (resulting in an agreement signed on August 8). Kosygin met Chou En-lai on September 11, the first high-level meeting for over four years; ambassadors were exchanged, thus contributing to this enterprise. At the same time, steady pressure was kept on China through the presence of forty divisions on their common frontier. Last but not least, the USSR would try to join forces with the United States after it had become aware of the Chinese danger.

This was the best, if not the only means at the disposal of the Soviet leaders to prevent an understanding between China and the US and, after the announcement of the presidential trip to Peking, they exploited every avenue in this direction. Well before this development, they had launched a campaign to open the eyes of the Americans to the Chinese threat and warn them of the risks involved in a rapprochement with China. In 1969, the USSR, according to H.R. Halderman, suggested to the Americans a joint operation aimed at the destruction of Chinese nuclear plants. For several months, there were reports of an imminent Soviet nuclear attack against China. Washington remained skeptical of the impact these rumors could have, but was anxious about the Soviet military build-up along the border with China. The USSR meanwhile lost no time in representing to the Americans that their approaches to China were felt to be "a thorn in the flesh." All these measures, meant to intimidate both the United States and China, but also indicating the possibility of real action (according to A. Shevchenko, this was seriously considered), were evidence of real anxiety. Only when talks with Washington started in earnest did Soviet fears become less intense.

The rapprochement between China and the US played a major part in starting the Soviet-American dialogue. Undoubtedly this was not the only factor: the wish to appear as a superpower, on a par with the United States, was a constant preoccupation of the Soviet leaders since Khrushchev's days. It was a matter of respectability as well as of power. The enterprise was hazardous: it was likely that the Third World would resent relations with the imperialists being given precedence over the "natural allies," the international communist movement would accuse the Soviets of neglecting their common interests, Eastern Europe would take advantage of this relaxation to regain some independence from "Big Brother." If the USSR was prepared to run these risks, it was not only because the Chinese threat gave it no choice and this policy was the most likely to bring about normalization, but also because it fitted in with previous foreign policy objectives and afforded a solution to serious internal problems.

Détente was beneficial to its western policy as a whole. It allowed progress in a direction which had always been of primary importance: achieving a split in the opposite camp and putting an end to a united front on the other side. The 1970-1971 agreements with Germany were a landmark in its policy regarding the West: they cleared the way towards détente while undermining American positions in Europe. They removed grounds for dispute and endless conflict between the two great powers in the post-war era in a region that was extremely sensitive for both. By endorsing the status quo brought about by the war, they confirmed the breakup of Europe into two parts and consequently the presence of the existing spheres of interest (a situation which would be corroborated a few years later by the Conference on Security and Cooperation in Europe). The crisis in Czechoslovakia and the military intervention had demonstrated the freedom of action of the USSR in the European socialist camp; the agreements on Germany, precisely because they resolved complicated problems went far beyond the scope of Germany, as well as making Soviet relations with the West more straightforward. Meanwhile the solution of these problems lessened European dependence vis-à-vis the US: one side could, if it so wished, distance itself from its powerful ally while the other was deprived of a trump card in Europe and had fewer reasons to intervene there. The Soviet-American rapprochement had every chance of making the process more marked and therefore weaken western cohesion.

If the USSR engaged fully in dialogue with Washington, it was partly for reasons of foreign policy. This policy also relieved grave internal difficulties: the economy was in deep trouble, seemingly of an intractable nature, and the country needed a new source of inspiration.

BALANCING THE SHORTCOMINGS
OF THE POLITICAL SYSTEM

Concerning the economy, the USSR no longer sought to achieve parity with the United States. The Brezhnev-Kosygin leadership was careful not to take up the slogan first uttered by Khrushchev: the objective of catching up and overtaking the Americans by 1970 in industrial production had not been realized. According to Soviet figures, in 1970 the GNP reached 65% of the American one and 66% in 1975; industrial production was 75% in 1970 and 80% in 1975.

What the USSR was now looking for was a remedy to its economic difficulties. The economy was slowing down: between 1951 and 1960 the yearly average rate of increase in the GNP was 5.8%; it was 5.1% between 1961 and 1970 and from 1971 to 1975 it fell to 3.7%. This decrease was a signal of alarm in the opinion of the Soviet leaders who were in the habit of declaring that the high rate of growth of their economy reflected the efficiency of their political system. It was all the more worrying as there was little that could be done to give a new impulse to the economy on the national level. Economic growth in the Soviet Union was based in the past on an increase in the labor-capital elements. Yet the Soviet leadership could rely less and less on the availability of labor to sustain growth, just at the time when the productivity of investments was in decline, when a proportionately larger share of those had to be allocated to agriculture and industries geared to consumer goods, i.e., sectors which do not contribute directly to the productive capability of industry.

Thus the Soviet leaders at the close of the 1960s had to adopt a more balanced policy for growth, based on increases in productivity, rather than growth in the input of labor and capital, i.e., an intensive type of growth rather than the previous extensive one. The problem lay in the fact that the yearly rate of growth in productivity was also getting lower: it went from 1.7% between 1950 and 1958, to 0.7% between 1958 and 1967 and -7% between 1967 and 1973. In order to improve it the Soviet leadership chose to draw resolutely on outside assistance. Since the Soviet Union had always been behind the West in advanced technology, trade with industrial countries and technological transfers were best suited to increase productivity through applying western techniques to industry: high quality equipment made it possible to satisfy internal demand faster.

The policy of turning to the West for help went hand-in-hand with a reappraisal of Soviet economic policy. Technological and economic independence, which tolerated outside contribution as necessary but temporary, was abandoned in favor of a policy of selective interdependence with western industrial countries. This realignment brought about a steady increase in the proportion of industrial capitalist countries in Soviet external trade, faster growth of trade with industrial countries than global external trade, and a larger share given to western technology in the 8th Plan and even more so in the 9th and 10th plans.

The policy of exchanges with the West constituted a full-blown economic program, its attraction being that it made it possible for the USSR to go on dispensing with fundamental economic reforms which would result in huge internal changes, and leaving both the needs of consumers and of heavy industry unaffected. This policy was also a way of exacerbating differences between industrial countries and having them compete with one another: trade was the best means to divide Western countries which had always found it difficult to coordinate their policies in this area.

Dialogue with Washington was vital to the decisions made by the Soviet leadership. A stable international environment was a condition for success in the task of "building socialism." If the two countries managed to control the arms race, the USSR would be able to allocate a reasonable share of its resources to military expenditure. Nobody knew exactly what the budget for the armed forces amounted to, but it was certainly very high (between 11 and 15% of the GNP according to various estimates, some dissidents making it as high as 40%), much higher than the American military budget.

These figures, however vague, give an idea of the serious inroads the military sector made into the Soviet economy and of the leaders' wish to reduce spending in this area.

From an economic point of view, the USSR, though it was not exclusively concerned with the Americans, was especially drawn to them because in many sectors the latter were technologically ahead. Because of the country's size and resources, US capability and habits were closer than those of Japan or European countries; as P.G. Peterson argued in 1972, the Soviet and American economies largely complemented each other, and the USSR had always admired American technology.

The slowdown in the economy, which might be followed by social unrest, the hidden consequences of the intervention in Czechoslovakia, plus increased competition with China at the close of the 1960s, created an atmosphere of decline in the USSR. The leaders were conscious of it and the Secretary General of the CPSU came under attack on this score between 1969 and the 24th Congress of the party (March-April 1971). To help the country retain its position in the world, difficulties which could not be avoided and for which there was no easy solution must be overcome somehow. One solution was found: stop trying to solve them, but go around them and forge ahead. This was what the Soviet leaders chose to do, foremost among them Leonid Brezhnev: opening the country to outside influence might prove, if successful, the best way to ease difficulties. This was the contribution détente was intended to make. Being treated as a power on a par with the United States, the USSR could impress the entire world, even the countries of Eastern Europe and its own citizens. This newly acquired status, consequent on its dealings with the US as a world power, helped to keep its brutal attack on Czechoslovakia in the background. Foreign policy became a tool for running internal policy. This was a fundamental prop of Brezhnev's platform which he made clear in the early 1970s: "Our external policy is the best instrument to deal with domestic affairs." Success abroad revived a greatly weakened political system and helped to make internal problems less alarming. This posture gave Soviet power a firm basis on which to spring back into action.

Thanks to his new policy, Brezhnev asserted his own authority. In 1970-71, the balance of power at the top shifted significantly to his advantage. From then on, he stood as *"primus inter pares."* He himself took care of foreign policy, while previously responsibility for it had been shared between Kosygin, Podgorny and him. Kosygin had looked after relations with the United States: he had met President Johnson at Glassboro in 1967, signed messages sent from the Soviet authorities to the American government and the Americans expected him to be in charge of further negotiations. Through 1970 and early in 1971, foreign affairs were gradually transferred to the Secretary General and, after the 24th Congress, all contacts between the US and the USSR went through him. At the first summit, he was the main interlocutor of Richard Nixon, which does not mean that he made all the decisions: during the talks, he always asked for his colleagues' advice and, before signing the SALT agreements, he called for a meeting of the Politburo. If he succeeded, after a few months, in asserting himself and taking precedence over the two other members of the "triumvirate," it was largely due to his insistence on the principle of opening up borders to outside influence. The 24th Congress, which laid down the main tenets of a "program for international peace and cooperation," later on to be invoked by Soviet leaders as being the basic principles of Soviet foreign policy, and spelled out the preeminence of the Secretary General, put a seal on the new direction taken, showing that Brezhnev had overcome earlier criticism. He now stood out as the man in charge of all negotiations with the USSR; having his country recognized as an equal by the greatest world power made his position unassailable.

Changes among Politburo members during the following months followed the new policy. In April 1973, Iu. Andropov, Chairman of the KGB, A.A. Grechko, Defense Minister and A. Gromyko, Foreign Minister, became full members, due to the links existing between these administrations and foreign affairs; meanwhile, the departure of P.E. Shelest and G.I. Voronov could be attributed to their hostility to the policy of détente advocated by the majority.

An examination of the importance given to foreign policy in the political system and of its connection with changes in the upper echelons of power give an idea of the price attached by Brezhnev and the country to Soviet-American dialogue. The fact that détente was the result of a deliberate choice on the part of the USSR explains why this policy, said to be irreversible, was so dear to them. Brezhnev emphatically made the point on many occasions, for example at Alma-Ata on August 15, 1973:

> A strikingly novel situation is developing in the international
> arena. [...] Détente has already brought about a whole system of
> treaties, agreements, and understandings which lay the founda-
> tions for peaceful and even constructive relations between
> socialist and capitalist countries. These developments allow us to
> hope that the present détente is not a flash in the pan, but the
> start of a fundamental reorganization of international relations.
> [...] The question now is how can we accelerate the process of
> détente, and make it irreversible.

A few months later, on March 15, 1974, he declared in the same
place: "In the last few years, something of enormous significance has
been achieved: a reversal in the course of foreign relations, a shift
from cold war to international détente...."

This was the idea expressed by Yevtuchenko in a poem entitled
"International détente," published in *Izvestia* on August 10, 1974,
just after President Ford's election:

> I am convinced that nobody will be able
> to separate America from Russia
> With a fresh flood of icy water...

Whether détente, a fundamental choice made by the USSR,
meant that relations with capitalist countries would be altered is not
certain. An analysis of the exact meaning attached to the word
détente may throw some light on this point.

A TRUCE WITH CAPITALISM?

The Soviet leaders saw détente above all as the building of a
material basis which was its apotheosis. They were convinced, like
the American analysts, that this material basis would create strong
links and incite the United States to cooperate. It would be strong
enough to overcome political difficulties, however serious; it would
underpin the new relationship and keep dialogue going. It would not
only ensure cooperation, but also the recognition of the USSR's new
international status, of its wish to be treated as an equal with joint
responsibility. Every effort therefore had to be made to enlarge the
scope of collaboration, to negotiate and reach agreements which
would form this material basis. According to the Soviet leaders, the
new climate of cooperation would serve the interests of both
countries: the USSR, they said, did not stand as beggars—its power
and resources made it potentially self-sufficient—but it did not wish

to live in autarchy and isolation. If the Soviets shared with the Americans a desire to develop cooperation in all directions and if they estimated also that it was a consequence of improving political relations, their appreciation rested on opposite premises. The Americans believed that the Soviet desire for cooperation stemmed from their need of the United States: they meant to use it as a lever if not as a weapon in negotiating. The Soviet leaders refuse to admit anything of the sort.

Détente was also a set of rules to be applied in the conduct of international relations. It was a complex, even ambiguous element of the Soviet analysis which presented two sides. On the one hand, the USSR declared that the superpowers must act with moderation; they had to prevent any given situation from escalating, i.e., leading to a breakup in exchanges. Such a notion was the basis for recognition of their joint responsibility in world affairs, and, implicitly, of spheres of influence, in Europe at least, as well as a certain complicity in their attitudes.

Yet, at the same time, the limits to be respected in international affairs remained undefined. They touched on physical and ideological boundaries which were apparent in the wording of the aims given to Soviet external policy at the time: peaceful cooperation with capitalist countries, strengthening of relations with socialist countries, strengthening of relations and contacts with countries breaking loose from the colonial yoke, assistance to all the peoples fighting for peace, for national liberation, democracy and socialism, and resistance to "all the actions of aggressive imperialist forces...." Between asserting that détente was not incompatible with the policy to be applied to the socialist bloc and the Third World and declaring that it must not stand in the way, there was only a short step. Regarding the socialist bloc, the situation was implicitly settled with the Americans. Things were not so straightforward concerning the Third World. The margin of error for the USSR, caught between the freedom of action it claimed as its right in certain areas of the world and its wish not to carry out a policy which might endanger their relations with the United States, was extremely narrow. On the one hand, the sharing of responsibilities (as, for example, in dealing with the Middle East, when the Geneva conference had all the parties concerned represented, together with the two great powers) enabled the Soviet leaders to feel officially recognized in world affairs and, like the American leaders, to act as the necessary intermediary for a solution to all major world problems. This was an achievement that no Third World ally should be able to endanger, as the preference given to the United States over Vietnam in May 1972 clearly showed. On the other hand, opening talks with the Americans did not lead to reconciliation; the USSR had to bear in mind the demands of the rivalry between two systems. The power of the Soviet Union had to be expressed both in dialogue with the United States and an active Third World policy. The Middle East would reveal the complexities of the two-pronged action.

The third element of Soviet thinking appeared there: détente was just a stage in the development of competition between the two systems. As Brezhnev explained:

> the class struggle of the two systems will continue in the sphere of the economy, politics and of course, ideology. It cannot be otherwise, since the world view and class aims of socialism and capitalism are opposed and cannot be reconciled. Yet we shall make sure that this necessary historical struggle does not develop a threatening character....

G. Arbatov, head of the Institute for the United States and Canada of the Academy of Science of the USSR, went on to explain that:

> the question is not whether the struggle between the two systems will continue or not. It lies in the forms the struggle will take. It can take various aspects, armed conflict, arms race, hot dangerous wars or peaceful coexistence: in this respect, the ideological struggle between the two systems, their competition in different fields go hand in hand with wide cooperation; inevitable disagreements can be solved through negotiations and a policy of arms limitation and disarmament replaces an all-out arms race.

The Soviet position, as explained on many occasions, was clear: détente was no truce, nor reconciliation, nor perfect understanding between the two countries. They remained in opposition. Each stayed the same: the USSR and the United States were the two major powers in the world, with conflicting social systems. The USSR was still the main opponent of imperialism. This was the reason why, even under the best circumstances, ideological struggle and competition (*sorevnovanie*) would continue because they were historically inevitable, but by peaceful means. Peaceful coexistence is a specific form of the class struggle. Sustained rivalry, however, was no barrier to peaceful solutions being sought in international problems or conflicts. This development, as the Soviets pointed out, was possible due to the powerful position of the USSR. The objective of détente was not to uphold the status quo. Dialogue was a stage in the course of competition, one which matched the characteristics of the present period and the needs of the USSR. The ultimate aim was an increase in Soviet power in all directions and simultaneously a weakening of American power.

From all Soviet official statements there was no doubt left: détente did not lead to any change in the nature of relations between the USSR and the capitalist countries, or the conflict between the two systems (on this point they were in agreement with the American analysis). From the very beginning, two facts clearly revealed their intention of improving the balance of forces on their side: constant strengthening of their strategic position and the efforts made to keep the characteristics of the Soviet state unaltered by détente.

Was strategic parity an objective for the USSR or merely a rung on the ladder to superiority? The question remained open at the time the first SALT agreements were signed, but it was soon answered. The Americans found out that the USSR, in the early 1970s, did not reduce military spending. An increase in defense resources was not in any case the only means at its disposal to alter the balance of power between the superpowers. Negotiations and SALT agreements had secondary effects in the United States—they encouraged pressures from public opinion against armament programs and fed a complex and lively debate which reduced the executive power's room for maneuver—and were likely to weaken the American position.

Regarding internal affairs, the stand of the USSR was clear: any interference in this area was incompatible with détente and no attack on the ideological basis of the USSR would be tolerated. There was no hope of it bringing in any internal relaxation, nor flexibility in relations with socialist countries. As the USSR feared its debilitating effects, it kept a sterner watch in respect to ideology and pressed harder for integration among the countries of the East European camp. In February 1966, the court appearances of the writers Daniel and Siniavski marked the start of a period of harsh repression against dissidents. This phenomenon, typical of the Brezhnev era, became more visible through the 1970s when links with the West were established. In 1973, the fact that Iu. Andropov, chairman of the KGB, was made a Politburo member (as candidate member) indicated that the Party remained vigilant and did not intend to loosen its grip on the population while détente made dangerous inroads in the ideology. The men in power had no intention of letting new ideas circulate following the movement of personnel due to normalization of relations with the US—all contacts therefore were kept to a minimum and newspapers made only vague reports on the links that were being established. Americans had limited freedom of movement in the USSR, not to be compared with the way Russians were treated in the United States and research scientists noticed that their Soviet counterparts were chosen much more for reasons of political beliefs than scientific ability, while they themselves were kept under strict surveillance in the USSR. Relations between Americans and Soviet dissidents were almost nonexistent. Every device was used to prevent meetings of this sort: thus, in June 1974, before President Nixon's visit, the Soviet authorities had the most notorious dissidents arrested (Jews foremost among them).

Yet if all the components of détente were taken into account and Soviet motivations examined, together with the practical consequences of the new policy, and the efforts that were made to apply it, the philosophy behind it was more complex than appeared at first sight. The USSR insisted on the fact that the nature of its relations with capitalist countries had not changed. Indeed détente was taking place within the framework of rivalry between the two systems, and the USSR's only aim was to strengthen its power and weaken that of the United States. But simultaneously, except during the war, the USSR never looked more like a nation-state among others, pursuing national objectives. It did not cut a revolutionary figure but appeared to be stable internally, reaching for normalization of its international status, trying to find a solution to its difficulties and make government more secure.

The intervention in Czechoslovakia in no way contradicted this principle, since it was intended to save a Soviet-type political system and the ensure the survival of the socialist camp, without which its power would vanish. The USSR's internal policy did not contradict it either. It was Soviet power which made détente possible. To prevent any criticism of this policy and of changes in international relations resulting from it, the USSR had to remain vigilant; anything that might threaten its power base had to be eliminated and all means of consolidating it had to be exploited. The best arena in which to do so was the military one. In other sectors, either it was difficult—this was especially true of the economy—or it would lead to an adverse reaction on the part of the United States, for example in pushing ahead too fast in Third World countries. The search for increased strategic capability derived also from the obligation of responding to the Chinese threat. Parity with the United States took no account of the Chinese factor. In 1972, there was no question of the United States and the USSR inviting China to participate in negotiations, as the country was too far behind. If, however, as seemed inevitable, Chinese defense capabilities were to develop, the superiority of the Soviets over their neighbor would disappear. The USSR was well aware of the danger.

The area of ideology was one where détente could most easily weaken the USSR. Both the USSR and Eastern Europe saw high risks as well as benefits in relations with the West. If the authorities were not careful, confrontation with the West might open the way for a show of independence on the part of those who had been exposed to capitalist influence. Their ideological monopoly might even be questioned, that is to say, the political system itself, which would be intolerable. Hence the need to buttress the legitimacy of the Party-based power system, to make sure that its dominance be recognized by everyone and to keep non-conformists and dissidents firmly under control.

Soviet leaders did not have much room to maneuver in this respect either, since they could not expect to be treated by the Americans as a respectable partner if their behavior at home was tyrannical. They tried their best to find more acceptable ways of dealing with rebels. Towards the late 1960s, they sought to improve the image of the police after the excesses of Stalin's era. In 1967, the KGB's prestige was enhanced by the appointment of a Central Committee secretary, i.e., a politician of the highest importance, as number one in the organization. Iu. Andropov's promotion to the Politburo was another sign of a change in policy. The KGB found a new respectability, not only in the quality of management, but also in the latest batch of recruits. Andropov made every effort to select an "intellectual elite" rather "doubtful elements," to improve its reputation and enable him to refine and diversify the methods used. The authorities cleverly resorted to every possible legal means in order to silence dissidents, a policy which proved highly successful. The campaigns of terror became things of the past, though imprisonment was still on the agenda. The fight against dissidents included such means as psychiatric internment, loss of Soviet citizenship, being expelled from associations (Writers' Union in the case of writers, for example), which were less objectionable to outside observers. For instance, in February 1974, Alexander Soljenitsyn was deprived of his nationality which, though devastating from his point of view, was more humane than being executed. Thus the leaders a way acquired a right of entry into the circle of civilized nations and prevented the US making aspersions on their internal policy.

A few months later, in August 1975, this new way of dealing with protest bore fruit and the final agreements were signed at Helsinki addressing cooperation in humanitarian processes. The fact that the USSR, together with countries belonging to the Western community, was signing a document which made the signatories guarantors of human rights and the free circulation of ideas and individuals, did not imply that the West would now be able to exert pressure in an area in which it had hitherto been forbidden to interfere, it was instead the consecration of its standing a par with other nation-states, and expecting, like its western partners, to be treated with consideration and respect.

It seems that détente brought in unsuspected changes in Soviet society. A process which started as a response to the need to form an alliance against China led to a kind of truce with the capitalist world. The USSR gained many advantages from this more relaxed attitude: being recognized as a great power, having its international status normalized, while its system could be protected from internal problems. Détente brought to the USSR a surge of dynamism, which had thus far been dormant, to such an extent that during the few months that it lasted there was some hope of seeing it extended. Maybe Nixon's idea of wrapping it in a web of cooperation would be successful?

9

DISAPPOINTMENTS

The pace of events was so fast that the question of détente was soon settled. As conditions for dialogue became clearer and the USSR discovered all the advantages attached to it, so did its limitations appear and a realization that it would be dangerous to exceed them.

DOUBTS AND DISAPPOINTMENTS IN THE MIDDLE EAST

The October 1973 war was the first serious crisis encountered by the superpowers since the thaw in their relations. It was a severe test for the policy of détente, whose results were far from satisfactory.

Richard Nixon had hoped that the new relations would incite the Soviet leaders to adopt a more moderate attitude in international affairs, especially in some sensitive regions of the world, making them less unstable. In the "Fundamental Principles," both parties admitted that "it was most important to prevent situations capable of souring their relations" and "any attempt made by either of them to gain, directly or indirectly, unilateral advantages to the detriment of the other was incompatible with the objectives" they had set for themselves. In the Middle East in 1973 the Americans wondered whether the USSR had not reneged on these principles.

Undoubtedly the Arabs were able to attack after reinforcing their positions because the USSR had given them military support before and after the conflict. They were provided with large quantities of modern weapons which thus far had only been delivered to Warsaw Pact countries (T-62 tanks, TU-22 bomber airplanes, SCUD rocket launchers) and Egyptian troops were trained by Soviet experts. By means of an airlift started early on the war, at a time when the Israelis were under great pressure, about 3,000 tons of equipment were dropped on the battlefield in less than a week. The USSR also gave constant encouragement through bellicose declarations and demonstrated that it was prepared to go to the brink when, on October 11, several airborne divisions were put on red alert and direct intervention was feared. On October 25, the United States put its troops on the alert. These factors indicate that, if the Soviet authorities did not incite Egypt and Syria to start hostilities, they made a war possible and in the early stages, the Arab front looked set to win. Because Soviet experts and their families were evacuated before the conflict started, it is obvious that they were in the know. The United States, on the contrary, was taken unawares, which means it had no advance warning from the other superpower. The declared objective of defusing crises had remained a dead letter.

Was this the end of détente? In order to answer this question, it is necessary to analyze Soviet attitudes. Détente was not meant to put a stop to competition between the superpowers, nor to bring about a realignment of alliances. The Middle East had been for a long time a favorite ground for Soviet activities in the Third World, while Egypt was the main point of anchorage and one of the earliest contacts for the USSR in this area. It had no intention of giving up its influence in this part of the world which would have meant abandoning long-term objectives in its power struggle. There was no question of ceasing to support its allies, although they had become much more demanding after the start of talks between the USSR and the US had made them suspicious. As H. Carrere d'Encausse pointed out, "the Arabs used the precedent of a Soviet withdrawal from Vietnam to peg their demands ever higher and question the validity of the USSR's support." The latter found itself "torn between relations with Washington, central to its formulation of the policy of détente, and the demands of its Arab allies." The contrary objectives of giving satisfaction to the Arabs so as not to appear as traitor to the Third World cause, and at the same time avoiding a conflict which might put détente at risk, made the position of the USSR extremely difficult.

Bearing in mind this dilemma, their decisions are easy to understand. On the one hand, the Soviet leaders gave generous aid to their allies, on the other they remained in touch with the American counterparts at all times. The Arabs were not given everything they asked for; later they argued that they had been provided with insufficient support in the conflict, not to be compared with their real needs. But their desire for revenge over Israel was such that they needed little encouragement to go to war. In June 1974, Brezhnev told Nixon that the Soviets had done their utmost to prevent the war breaking out, but they had been unable to defuse the situation. There may be some truth in the assertion.

Support to the Arabs went hand-in-hand with determination to keep a dialogue going with the United States; this is why the conflict could be contained within the framework of détente. The Soviet leaders never lost sight of the necessity of dialogue, although it did not always coincide with harmony and understanding of each other. It really amounted to negotiations taking place in a situation of extreme fluidity. When the USSR pressed Kissinger to come to Moscow to survey the development of the Middle Eastern war, it was on October 19, a desperate time from the Egyptian point of view. Yet consultations had never been interrupted. The last talks proved useful, as the superpowers managed to negotiate a cease-fire in Moscow on October 22. The crisis which erupted on October 25 in no way contradicts this point. Carrere d'Encausse viewed the events in this way: what the USSR did in these three days which startled the United States into declaring a state of red alert

> constitute[d] a remarkable example of relations at the top using a new medium. The steps taken were intended to show the United States that the Soviet position was untenable. The way the Americans reacted proved that the message had been received. The nuclear alert made it possible for the USSR to back down without losing face. Far from signaling a breakdown in Soviet-American relations, the crisis of October 25, 1973, was in fact an example of the way they worked. [...] The complicity that developed between Moscow and Washington, the uninterrupted contacts between the leaders of the two countries were enough for the USSR to feel sure that things would not escalate and get out of hand.

The fact that pressure from the United States prevented Soviet troops being sent to the Middle East made the benefits of dialogue clear over the long-term. It was a setback for the USSR, but not a defeat, since the crisis ended with the armies laying down their arms before the Egyptians had been beaten out of existence by the Israelis.

The USSR seems to have acted with moderation in this conflict. Henry Kissinger declared on October 12, at the end of the first week of fighting: "We do not consider [...] that the Soviets have shown to any degree the lack of responsibility which could, as I have said before [...] endanger détente." His opinion was not greatly altered by the October 25 crisis. "Détente did not prevent a crisis occurring," he wrote in his *Memoirs*, but it should be remembered that the latter "did not signify friendship, but rather a strategy to be applied to relations between opponents. [...] Détente made less acute the series of crises which the differing ideologies and geopolitical interests rendered almost inevitable." On January 30, 1974, Richard Nixon declared in the State of the Union address: "The strength of détente has been sorely tried," but he did not think the crisis would put an end to relations with the USSR as defined in the policy of détente outlined during the 1972 and 1973 summits. Many American journalists and parliamentarians (Senator Jackson among them) were less sanguine. They found the posture of the USSR highly disturbing and blamed the president for lack of firmness in defense of détente. Public opinion was no longer convinced of the soundness of a policy which had lost much of its prestige.

In Moscow, the crisis and its consequences had more serious effects. Since it brought about an unfavorable situation for the USSR, the development of the policy of détente had reached a watershed. The USSR had conceived of détente as a system of consultations resulting from its superpower status. In the Middle East, it sought a settlement reached with arbitration from the great powers after negotiations had taken place under their guarantee. It refused to be kept away from the negotiating table while the United State presided and basked in glory. In 1967, the Soviets had kept on the sidelines. Now, with détente as a backdrop, they felt responsible together with the United States in settling the conflict. This participation would enhance their role as intermediaries in the disputes between the various local states, among them Israel; it would add legitimacy to their interest in this part of the world and put a seal on their status as a great power guaranteeing the terms of the agreement.

This war, in which the USSR stood within firing range from both sides, torn between its desire to keep the talks with the United States uninterrupted and to help its allies, the Arab states, so as to appear as a necessary partner, made its position most uncomfortable. Early on, though, the conflict did not seem to have too many drawbacks from the Soviet point of view. On the contrary, it could wipe out the memory of their poor performance in 1967 and bring into relief their part in protecting Arab interests against Israeli encroachment. If the war turned out to the advantage to the Arab side, as seemed likely during the early stage of fighting, much to the astonishment of the Americans, it would be thanks to Soviet assistance, not through an American intervention. There was every hope therefore that, in the process, the position of the USSR in the region would be strengthened both vis-à-vis the Arabs and the Americans, who would not be able to negotiate without Soviet participation. The peace conference, to be held in Geneva, was a welcome development because it brought together the parties involved and the two super-powers round the negotiating table.

The USSR soon realized that, in spite military successes on the Arab side, events did not confirm earlier expectations: the October war led to a rapprochement between Egypt and the United States who gained more sway in the Middle East. The USSR could exert its influence only on the Arabs, while it was imperative to make Israel yield some ground. Since the United States was the one who could put pressure on the latter until it understood the need for dialogue with the Arabs, its influence proved irresistible. As soon as the conflict ended, the Egyptians, far from feeling grateful towards the USSR, turned to the Americans whom they firmly believed would be able to advance their cause: an announcement that diplomatic relations would be restored was made on November 7. Soon discussions started between Arabs, Israelis and Americans. With the signing of an Israel-Egypt agreement, called the Km101 agreement, on November 11, it was clear that the balance of power had shifted in favor of the United States. The Geneva conference, with both superpowers taking part, proved disappointing: it set up an Israeli-Egyptian study group whose task was to resume negotiations under the authority of the United Nations, but those negotiations ended in failure. The Secretary of State went on to-ing and fro-ing in the Middle East and managed to wrench an agreement from the Egyptians, signed on January 17, 1974, in the guise of an interim arrangement and a few months later, on September 4, 1974, the Israelis agreed to sign the second Sinai agreement with Egypt. On the Syrian front a document was signed on May 31, 1974, which put a seal on Israeli-Syrian withdrawal from the Golan. This successful outcome proved that the Americans were capable of acting as go-between in the Middle East and settling a conflict without Soviet participation.

The USSR did not remain idle in the face of these American advances. As it was clear that Kissinger's policy of step-by-step agreements was not likely to achieve an overall settlement, in the months following the end of the war the Kremlin advocated global negotiations, emphasizing the fact that piecemeal agreements guaranteed by one superpower were useful in the short-term only. They never tired of demanding a resumption of the Geneva conference, with the two world powers sitting as equals to find a way of reaching a global settlement "which would take into account the interests of any third party" and would be guaranteed by them. Nothing came of these efforts. The years 1974 and 1975 were marked by Kissinger's successes, increased American influence in the region, and Egypt's definite shift away from Moscow towards Washington.

What the Soviet leaders noticed was that the Americans had left them out in their effort to find a settlement. Each time there was a possibility for the latter to act on their own, throughout the crisis and later—they dramatized things so as to be able to reject sending an American-Soviet force on the spot—they did so, taking care afterwards to emphasize their role in the final settlement. The Middle East had previously been a battle ground for rivalry between the superpowers. Détente, much to the USSR's disappointment, did not alter the situation. This attitude on the part of the American leaders was felt as a rebuff: the United States had no intention of sharing power and responsibility with the Soviets. The Americans accepted parity and looked for a balance of power between them, yet as soon as an opportunity presented itself, they did not hesitate in settling one of the most serious conflicts of the period on their own, reducing the part played by the USSR in the negotiations, until the Soviets lost most of their influence in the area. It was a matter not of containment, but rather rolling-back Soviet power.

The USSR had attempted to accommodate mutually exclusive demands: it had chosen détente in the hope that it would facilitate the growth of its influence, that its cooperation with the United States would give legitimacy to its activity in the region. In fact, the new policy brought few rewards in its wake: the conflict ended with its position in a highly sensitive area seriously weakened. For the Soviet leaders this was a turning point in the course of détente and they questioned its usefulness as well as the wisdom of moderation in dealing with the United States, if the latter, instead of being influenced by it, took advantage and undermined their power.

SOVIET RESPECTABILITY UNDER ATTACK

The Soviet leaders' doubts increased as they knew that voices were heard in the United States at the time to question the respectability of their country and the American government found it impossible to silence them. The USSR became suddenly aware that the United States had acknowledged its power but stopped short of showing respect as well and, furthermore, President Nixon's policy of détente was not unanimously approved by the population.

When two governments respect each other, they discuss problems and make joint decisions without looking into the other's internal affairs if these do not affect the other party. Even more so, a government cannot demand changes in a given area of the other's internal policy if it is not directly involved. International dealings are conducted largely on these principles of equality and non-interference, principles that Soviet and American leaders endorsed as a basis for dialogue and to which the former gave the highest importance.

From the beginning, the Nixon government had declared that its strategy made it imperative to accept the USSR as it was. The question was not whether or not it wished to see the USSR introduce reforms in its internal policy; rather it did not think it possible to simultaneously influence the Kremlin's internal and external policies, hence its determination to focus its attention on moderating Soviet behavior in international affairs. Undoubtedly some of the attitudes of the USSR did not meet with its approval, especially its disregard for basic human rights, but it was convinced that these matters had to be kept separate from the policy of détente and that, in any case, unofficial diplomatic action was the only really effective way of acting. It fully intended to put pressure on certain humanitarian points, but in a discreet manner, through the new personal relations established with Soviet leaders. As President Nixon explained on June 5, 1974, in a speech delivered at Indianapolis: "We serve our ideals best by being concerned with results," and further on: "We shall obtain more results through diplomatic action than through hundreds of eloquent speeches."

In the atmosphere of optimism generated by détente in the United States, this guiding principle had not been questioned. In the summer of 1973 more attention was paid to its validity. It was highly embarrassing for the Americans to have their policy become a subject for debate and the Soviet leaders dreaded the consequences of this public display of doubt. Both governments were appalled to hear the demands made by Congress, and supported by a significant number of ordinary Americans, for a liberalization of Soviet internal policy.

"On the whole, Congress approves of détente," Senator A. Ribicov declared in 1975. But Congress, using its constitutional power to make most-favored-nation status conditional on emigration of Soviet citizens—that is, making commerce serve political ends—

prevented the 1972 trade agreement from taking effect and deprived Nixon of a significant element of his strategy. This strategy was based on the executive being able to allow, or deny trade with the Soviet Union, looking on it as a lever to encourage or punish the other according to its international conduct and its observance of signed agreements. The episode of the 1974 Trade Act showed that the executive did not enjoy this power.

The affair started when, following a Soviet decree passed in August 1972, which introduced taxes on all people who wished to emigrate after receiving higher education, Senator H. Jackson presented the American Senate in October 1972 with an amendment by which the President twice a year would have to give Congress an assurance that the countries benefiting from the status of most-favored-nation did not impose abnormal restrictions on emigration. After a long and heated debate in Congress and in the public at large, with the media giving the problem a large coverage, the amendment was passed in January 1975.

Jackson, to start with, was backed by some 70 senators, but he found support in the House of Representatives in C. Vanik, a member of the powerful Ways and Means Committee. In 1973 Vanik presented two amendments, one forbidding the application of the most-favored-nation clause to any communist country unless the President gave an assurance to Congress that the said country did not prevent emigration, the other refusing to give credit through Exlmbank to countries curbing emigration. Although the second amendment was not passed by the Committee, they were both presented to the House of Representatives which approved them in December 1973. In the Senate the affair dragged on through 1974 in the hands of the Finance Committee. Kissinger, dreading the consequences these amendments would have if they were passed, looked for a compromise with Senate on the one hand and the Soviet leaders on the other. On October 18, 1974, the Secretary of State and the Senate reached an agreement: the latter announced that it would lift restrictions in exchange for the government giving assurances on Soviet emigration policy. The compromise, according to Senator Jackson, was based on the assumption that the USSR's yearly emigration rate would increase from the 1973 level (about 35,000 people) and would match the number of applications, which in his estimation was 130,000 plus; the figure of 60,000 would be taken as minimum.

On the basis of this compromise, Senator Jackson presented a fresh amendment: the Senate adopted it unanimously (88 voted for, against 0), and on December 13 approved the Trade Act. On December 18, the very day both Houses reached an agreement on the matter, *Pravda* published a declaration sent by the Tass Agency refusing to admit that assurances had been given by the USSR on a liberalization of its emigration policy in exchange for trade concessions made by the United States; the whole thing was described as gross interference in internal affairs. *Pravda* also published a letter sent on October 26 by Andrei Gromyko to Henry Kissinger, in which he stated that the letters exchanged between Jackson and Kissinger on October 18, dealing with conditions to be observed by the USSR, gave a distorted picture of the Soviet position. The Soviet reaction is easy to understand since on December 3, Kissinger recognized in the Senate that any assurances he had given in October were based not on any "formal agreements" made by the Soviets, but on explanations they had provided regarding their emigration policy.

In the terms of the Trade Act, approved by Congress (by a large majority with some 80% of votes) on December 20, the president was allowed to grant the status of most-favored-nation to communist countries, on condition they put no limitations on emigration. He had permission to waive the restriction over a period of eighteen months if he received an assurance from the country concerned that its policy would be directed towards freedom of emigration from then on and kept Congress informed of further development. After eighteen months, an extension of the granting of the clause by dispensation would be submitted to Congress for approval. Government credit was also restricted under these conditions.

The Trade Act was signed by President Ford on January 3, 1975. Ten days later, on January 14, Kissinger announced that the Soviets had rejected the clauses of the law applying to them. The consequences of this rejection were far-reaching: the 1972 trade agreement could not become effective. The USSR therefore could not benefit from the status of most-favored-nation, nor could it qualify for Exlmbank credit and the settlement of Lease-Lend was suspended once more. Normalization of trade relations between the two countries had miserably failed.

The USSR put severe restrictions on every person wishing to emigrate, but more especially on Jews, who had largely received a university education. There was nothing new in the United States paying particular attention to their treatment, nor to linking the fate of Jews with the clause of most-favored-nation. In 1837, Russia and the United States had signed a treaty granting the status to Russia, but the American government had declared it null in 1911 to protest the tsar's policy vis-à-vis Russian Jews.

In 1970, the American Congress had already voiced its disquiet at the discriminatory treatment inflicted on Russian Jews. But its activities in 1972-1974 went far beyond the Jewish problem. They rested on the principle that détente could not come in installments: it came as a package. The Soviets could not enjoy its benefits without suffering consequences. Congress was opposed to the American government conducting a policy of dialogue and cooperation with the USSR while remaining blind to internal affairs, especially in respect to human rights violations which remained largely ignored; it was thought that, thus far, the United States had, in this respect, given too much and received too little. A letter received from Andrei Sakharov on September 14, 1973, in support of the Jackson Amendment confirmed this belief. The celebrated academician went further: in 1974, at a time when Nixon was on an official visit in Moscow, he started a hunger strike to attract the attention of the American public to the plight of dissidents in the Soviet Union.

The action taken by Congress was also motivated by a basic imbalance in the matter of most-favored-nation status: the Soviet government controlled every aspect of trade, so the fact that the United States granted right of entry to its products in no way guaranteed American products free access to the Soviet market. There being no question of reciprocity, Congress felt entitled to ask for something in exchange, if need be, in a political matter. This attitude was partly due to relations with the executive being at a low ebb: it was an opportunity to curb the government's initiatives in many areas. Senator Ribicov explained it this way: "It would compel the Executive regularly to account to Congress on the subject of USSR-US economic links, regarding their nature and range...."

As the debate became increasingly demagogic, with few Congressmen wishing to be accused of "giving dollars more importance than freedom" or to annoy their Jewish electors who were present in large numbers in certain states, the supporters of human rights in the USSR joined forces with all opponents of détente in general, thus creating a formidable coalition. Voices were heard at the time (1973), even among some of Nixon's sympathizers, on the question of the psychological consequences to détente: might there be a risk of it weakening American determination, and how long could containment go hand-in-hand with cooperation? This outcry was the result of deep-seated uneasiness in the American public.

The government did not attract criticism only on this controversial subject; there were many people who condemned Congress for acting in a clumsy, illogical, and inefficient way. Business circles in particular were angry seeing the negative effect the Act would have on commercial exchanges. Opinion polls gave a figure of 86% of American companies as hostile to the Jackson Amendment and 83% supporting the application of the most-favored-nation clause to the USSR without preconditions. The AFL-CIO also opposed Congress on this point, but for different reasons: the trade unions advocated more protectionist legal measures. Impartial observers pointed out how irrational it was to take punitive action against the USSR for its internal policy while other countries, which showed no more respect for human rights, were still enjoying American support. The government had no doubts about it and was emphatic in its disapproval. "We must be under no illusions as to the character of the Soviet system, but we must not err in our dealings with the USSR," President Ford told Congress on April 10, 1975. The law "was not only harmful to our relations with the Soviet Union"; it resulted in letting Western Europe and Japan enter markets "which would otherwise have gone to the Americans"; and "it also seriously compromised the chances of aspiring emigrants." As a matter of fact, the number of Jews allowed to leave the USSR, which had risen from 400 yearly in 1968 to 35,000 in 1973 (mostly following unofficial pleas made by the American government) dropped significantly later on: 21,000 in 1974, between 13,000 and 17,000 from 1975 to 1977; only in 1978 did the figure climb again for the first time since 1974.

Not surprisingly, seeing how touchy they were on the subject, the Soviets' reaction was quick: they denounced the amendment on frequent occasions and in the most violent terms. On principle, they refused to use trade as a counter in politics and establish a link between trade and other sectors which should be kept separate. They declared this artificial connection poisonous for relations between them an inhibitor in growth of commercial exchanges which were destabilized. There was no way the United States could be regarded as a trustworthy partner. In this instance, they saw the most-favored-nation/freedom of emigration linkage as unacceptable interference in internal affairs and a refusal to respect principles on which the USSR and the United States had agreed to build inter-state relations.

It was a concern they found entirely negative as it contradicted a basic principle in international life, at least among western countries—non-interference in the internal affairs of other nation-states. The USSR had thought itself accepted in the western international community because of its power, like any other member, i.e., a civilized and respectable nation-state which would be treated accordingly. The fact that, as soon as an opportunity arose, the United States blamed it for some aspect of its internal policy and required internal regulations to be altered using economic concessions as an argument proved that a mistake had been made: the Americans acknowledged Soviet power, since they had no choice anyway, but they continued to regard it as an outcast whose behavior had to be watched. Blaming its emigration policy meant casting a doubt on its honesty, denying it any respectability. Refusing to grant the status of most-favored-nation, from the Soviet point of view, made American demands exorbitant. To the Soviet leaders' minds, the clause was neither a concession, nor a privilege, but the recognition of equal status, a normal procedure for a country's commercial partners: it was a non-discriminatory regime, widely accepted in international trade, applied as a matter of course to their commercial partners by the US; it was a symbol of normalized relations, similar to diplomatic relations, which constituted a test for American willingness to develop economic relations with the USSR. Thus not to most-favored-nation status it was a demonstration of ill-will.

It had been thought that consideration, the crowning of its international achievements and new-found power, had finally been recognized as its due. But in reality, in comparison with other developed countries, unequal treatment was meted out to the USSR, exactly as in the past. From the American leaders' declarations it seemed that they would not attempt to transform the Soviet internal system—this aspect of American policy had been most appealing—it was logical to deduct that the country would be judged on its power (an element it could depend on) and no longer on its internal organization, which in any case had been made to look less objectionable to the outside world. It turned out that détente was now used as a way to put pressure on the Soviet Union. It was also to be expected that if the Americans today dared to raise the question of emigration, tomorrow they would demand something else to be put right. The

USSR came to the conclusion that either there was a breakdown in the established policy or there had been a misunderstanding from the beginning. This conditional détente which sprang up out of the blue was unacceptable. The superpower could not allow anyone to meddle into its internal affairs, to appreciate whether or not it was on the right course. Détente meant mutual recognition of the need to live in peace—no charge should be exacted for upholding it.

Besides, the Americans made so much of the affair that the USSR could not give in without losing face. Freedom of emigration for the Jews was part of a whole picture: relations with Arab countries were affected since the latter were angry over Soviet Jews swelling the ranks of their enemies. The cohesion of the Soviet empire was also involved: why allow, at least on principle, Jewish emigration, if you refuse the same thing to other nations? Economic considerations came in also: Moscow claimed that the measures taken by Congress were highly damaging to them. Limitation of credit was certainly so, but the matter of import costs was different. It is not likely that those weighed heavily in the position taken by the Soviets. They considered the matter essentially political.

What made the situation worse, from their point of view, was that the American government was unable to control it, however much it tried. The fact that Congress passed an amendment which put at risk a key element of Nixon's strategy put into high relief the narrow confines within which the leadership could maneuver. It showed the American executive with little freedom of movement, making decisions which could be reexamined by Congress at any time. This was a political reality which, so far, the Soviet leaders had remained unaware of, but now was blocking the way ahead. The American authorities were no longer dependable, the Soviets suddenly realized. The affair had not developed as a reaction to other problems; it arose in 1972, when détente had reached its climax, and it was self-sufficient. It indicated that détente, as conceived by Nixon and his associates, was not approved unanimously in the United States: the opponents of this dialogue with Moscow, who had remained silent in the euphoric atmosphere of the summit meetings, became more vocal as soon as an opportunity arose and the executive power was unable to contain criticism. No better illustration could be found of the "anti-détente forces" (as the Soviet expression goes) raising their heads suddenly and defeating the government's policy.

Thus the Jackson amendment had repercussions far beyond questions of emigration and trade arrangements: it caused a deep rift in détente both in the United States and in the USSR. The American Congress did not wish to abandon dialogue, but rather improve its quality. Yet by choosing to act as it did, it deprived the government of a "carrot," a means to incite the Soviets to be mindful of American interests, and it upset the current strategy. The turmoil that followed blew the whole thing out of proportion and cut short much needed reflection on the basic difficulties to resolve in super-power relations. The right to emigrate was, naturally, a fundamental problem, just as questions related to the economy were of great importance, but undoubtedly Soviet-American relations were not limited to emigration and trade and the course taken by the Nixon government (exerting discreet pressure in favor of human rights) was probably as valid as any other.

The USSR reached a turning-point when the affair broke: respectability, which had been considered as finally recovered and the great, if not the main, advantage of rapprochement with the United States, was put in the balance again. It became obvious that the Nixon government did not carry enough weight, that it could not silence its critics and impose its policies. In 1973-74, bitter disappointment set in: détente had led to a weakening of the Soviet position in the Middle East and to a successful American campaign to exclude the country from international society. Was it worth it ?

AMERICAN EXECUTIVE POWER IN A STATE OF COLLAPSE

Washington soon made the answer clear. At a time when the Soviet leaders were wondering about the wisdom of carrying on with dialogue, the Americans, through their actions, altered conditions so drastically that unmistakable conclusions had to be drawn. Just when difficulties had to be ironed out around the negotiating table, the USSR watched incredulously as the American executive floundered in a sea of internal trouble until he finally drowned. This situation was bound to have serious consequences, not only because the United States was no longer able to pay attention to Soviet concerns and take them into account, but also because the balance of forces, on which détente rested, was upset. Dialogue requires equilibrium between two sides. If one of the parties faded away, the balance was affected and it was easy to guess that the other would take advantage of the situation. As it happened, the other had every reason to benefit from the breakdown.

On August 8, 1974, about two years after a burglary that took place at the headquarters of the Democratic Party, the Watergate building, in Washington, on June 17, 1972, the President was forced to resign. A simple burglary unleashed a huge political scandal which shook the entire body politic for months to come and ended, on October 10, 1973, with President Nixon being impeached, the Vice-President, Spiro Agnew, resigning, as well as several of their close associates having to bow out.

From the Soviet point of view, the Watergate affair was inconceivable and the leaders may not have fully understood it, since it was only possible under a political system completely alien to theirs. They must have agreed with the opinion expressed by an experienced person (in the summer of 1973) that it was only play-acting and that Nixon could easily have remained in power if he had tried harder, as revealed in an article published on November 3, 1974, in *The New York Times*. To start with, they did not pay much attention to it, seeing it as another internal struggle for power. Such a struggle concerned them insofar as they believed it to be fueled by a sector of public opinion which opposed Nixon's policy, especially regarding détente, but they did not take it very seriously. In 1972 and 1973, the Soviet press hardly mentioned Watergate, qualifying it as a purely internal affair and left the name of Nixon largely out of it. After the second summit, they had to change their attitude since it loomed too large to ignore.

On the day when the Soviet delegation arrived in the United States, in a press conference Archibald Cox, the special prosecutor, stated that he was looking into the possibility of President Nixon being charged, even before the declaration of impeachment had been made. The statement to be made by John Deane, ex-legal adviser to the White House, to a commission headed by Senator Erwin, would have coincided with Brezhnev's visit and was postponed by a week. But the proceedings were resumed on the last day of the Soviet leader's stay, so the latter was able to witness the public indictment of his American counterpart. Being shown at close quarters the turmoil raised by Watergate was a shock for these men molded by a political system as secretive and authoritarian as the Soviet one, who were also the leaders of the "opposite camp." They listened in amazement to the news of the greatest world power being torn apart, in full view of its opposite number and they felt great anxiety about the future. This display of questionable behavior made them unsure of the stability of American executive power, of its capacity to tackle problems and they wondered about the likelihood of the "anti-détente forces" getting the upper-hand again. Did they draw their conclusions there and then? Did the affair have any relation with the October war breaking out? Under different circumstances would they have tried harder to calm down their bellicose Arab allies? Perhaps, but nothing is less certain. Having very high expectations of an ongoing dialogue, they did not wish at the time to endanger it by an operation which exceeded the demands of their alliance with Arab countries.

Nixon's resignation one year later, when the Soviet leaders had made an evaluation of the advantages brought on by détente, demonstrated to them that the "anti-détente forces" had won the day in the United States. It was also the death-knell of face-to-face political deals. If Nixon, who had made of rapprochement with the USSR one of the guidelines of his foreign policy and had achieved spectacular results, had failed in his enterprise, who else would succeed? They also understood that the resignation of the United States' President was itself such an upheaval and the expression of such profound unrest that the country would not recover quickly from it, especially in the context of the Vietnam war, which was becoming increasingly unpopular.

For ten years, the Americans had been fighting a war in Vietnam which soon attracted a great deal of criticism. After 1965-66, they found it hard to understand the reasons for their action, especially since results proved disappointing. It was a costly war which offered little prospect of ending successfully in the near future, in spite of government promises. The most powerful country in the world could not bring a little Asian country to admit defeat; neither could it bring it to negotiate. The negotiations that started in May 1968 dragged on for four years to no effect. When the peace agreement was finally signed, on January 27, 1973, relations between the United States and North Vietnam remained strained and the situation on the spot very difficult. The war left Americans skeptical of the role their country could play in the world, and the national mood inclined towards isolationism once more.

The horrors of a dirty war, the debilitating effect it had on the presidential office and the opposition between executive and legislative powers (due not so much to the fact that the president was a Republican while Congress had a Democratic majority, but rather to Nixon governing without sufficiently taking the latter into account) incited the House of Representatives to significantly curb the president's power. On July 1, 1973, an amendment to the Financial Law was passed which prevented the president to use, after August 15, 1973, the sums earmarked for the Defense Department to be spent on the war effort in Indochina. On November 7, 1973, it adopted a law preventing the president from entering another conflict of his own accord: from then on, he was only allowed to send troops abroad under specific conditions and he had to inform Congress within 48 hours. If Congress did not vote for a declaration of war, the president had to withdraw his troops within 60 to 90 days. Later on, Congress extended its power further at the expense of the president by tightening its control over the budget and instituting the right of veto over the application of a law already passed and, if need be, the right to amend the wording of a law.

About this time, the power of the CIA was severely curtailed after the organization had been accused of exceeding its rights, of providing misinformation on Vietnam, and using ill-chosen means to achieve its ends; thus the Intelligence Agency lost much of its efficiency and the executive was deprived of an valuable weapon.

If the Soviet leaders had remained, in 1974-75, in some doubt as to the damages inflicted on the US by the Vietnam war and Watergate, the American attitude in Vietnam and Africa would soon open their eyes.

The Americans had declared repeatedly that they would not let the USSR take advantage of the policy of détente to thwart western interests. They would be quick to react if relaxation of tension was used as a cover to exacerbate local conflicts in unstable parts of the world and they would oppose any attempt by the USSR to rise to a position of superiority, either on a global or regional scale, preserving at all times their means to carry out a chosen policy. In the end, when détente had come to a standstill and the United States had to make a decisive move, it remained paralyzed.

In his report on foreign affairs dated May 3, 1973, Nixon declared that the United States would keep a watchful eye on the situation and would not tolerate an infringement of the Paris agreement concerning Vietnam. He warned Hanoi that North Vietnam would risk a fresh confrontation with the United States if the agreements were not respected, or if they served to extend its influence in South Vietnam. Two years later, in April 1975, Saigon surrendered unconditionally to the Communist troops. Henceforth there would be one Vietnam, under a communist regime. Before the collapse, the South Vietnamese had reminded the Americans of their promises, to no avail. When the May 3, 1973, report was published, the Americans were almost sure that the North Vietnamese were not being honest and continued to infiltrate the South with men and materiel. As time went on, this truth became increasingly clear. Yet how could the president react at a time when Congress had deprived him of any effective means of counteracting the communist campaign and had decided not to engage in any new foreign venture? "We have denied ourselves all legal means to enforce the agreements, thus giving North Vietnam every assurance that it could violate them with total impunity," President Ford declared on April 10, 1975, immediately before the North Vietnamese offensive, and went on to say that Hanoi had systematically violated the Paris agreement from the very day it was signed. He then asked Congress to act and grant South Vietnam emergency military aid, so that, among other things, the free nations of Asia could not think "that the United States are shrinking from their obligations or intend to abandon them if they come under attack." "We cannot hope to see the Soviet Union act with moderation," he went on, showing great perspicacity, "if the United States prove weak and hesitant."

The same pattern applied to Africa in the same year. After the decision taken by Portugal, in 1974, to give its overseas territories their independence, power in Angola officially devolved to a four-party interim government (the metropolitan government and the three nationalist movements—the MPLA, FNLA and UNITA) until independence was declared in November 1975. The USSR had backed the MPLA since the early 1960s, but it increased its support in 1974-75, when clashes between the three movements degenerated into civil war. Under the circumstances, the American leadership decided to give unofficial financial support to the FNLA and UNITA, to the tune of $32 million in 1975. This initiative came to a sudden halt, late in 1975, when it became known. Congress did not approve of it and on January 27, 1976, formally ruled against it, in spite of the Secretary of State's representations; the latter unsuccessfully pointed out that the United States' vital interests were at risk (access to raw materials and waterways) and to remain a world power it had to oppose the Soviet intervention by force. From then on, the American government had to be content with addressing verbal warnings to the USSR—to no effect—and canceling or postponing conferences, such as those of the Energy, Trade and Habitat Commissions which were to take place in the spring of 1976.

Congress' rejection of US involvement in Africa (that is to say, of the risks inherent to any intervention), appeared to the Soviet leaders as giving them the "green light": their African policy was without danger since the Americans did not oppose it. No longer fearing confrontation with the United States, they were free to launch a large-scale intervention in Angola. According to Henry Kissinger, the American aid sent to Angola in the summer and autumn of 1975 prevented the MPLA having the run of the whole country on November 11, the day when it became independent, and made it possible for the other parties to take a determined stand against the Soviet-Cuban intervention. After a warning from President Ford, on December 9, the USSR suspended its air-lift until December 24. Following the Senate's decision to stop all assistance to the FNLA and UNITA, the USSR resumed its military support, while Cuba (which in October 1975 had started sending troops to support the MPLA on the spot) sent twice as many men. Their support was decisive and allowed this movement to gain the upper-hand over its rivals. As soon as Angola became independent, Moscow developed relations and, in October 1976, signed a treaty of friend-ship and cooperation (as it had done with India and Egypt in 1971), which was reinforced by an agreement between the Soviet Union's Communist Party and the MPLA.

Soviet intervention in Angola projected a new light on the power of the USSR as it now extended much beyond its traditional sphere of interest. The American public was deeply shocked by this Soviet show of aggression in the field of foreign policy. Their hopes were dashed, probably forever, by the support given to Angola, as well as to other ex-Portuguese territories (Mozambique in particu-lar), by the USSR and its Cuban ally. The Americans had counted on their policy of cooperation and dialogue to prompt the Soviets to take a softer line on the international stage. They had to admit instead that the latter preferred to put these new relations in jeopardy for the sake of increasing their power in the Third World. Their interpretation of recent events was clear: the Soviet leaders took advantage of détente to become the dominant partner. Was this true?

Were they not rather taking advantage of the American executive losing its authority at a time when relations with Washington were proving disappointing?

Between 1973 and 1975, Nixon's strategy lost its direction; gradually all the levers disappeared. Within a few months, the president was denied the possibility of encouraging the USSR through economic agreements or punishing any imprudent moves that might be made. Nixon's strategy relied on firmness and conciliation; as soon as the USSR overstepped the boundaries set by the United States and détente had reached its limits, the latter had to react strongly and show determination. Instead the US adopted a submissive attitude and the whole strategy came unwound.

In order to make effective use of firmness and conciliation, the White House needed the approval of the American populace, the government services and Congress. This was not the case. Richard Nixon's room to maneuver was restricted to start with, until it finally became impossible for him to take action because his policy was not the result of a compromise between the executive and the other branches of government. The impetus of détente made the groups interested in cooperation with the USSR, such as business, urge the development of cooperation. Yet the strained internal situation brought a disruptive confrontation between Congress and the president. In comparison, the USSR had an enormous advantage because of its authoritarian political system: the executive power made all the decisions in foreign policy, without taking account of any other body or of public opinion.

Nixon's strategy was conditional on a mood of buoyancy, but when the United States was no longer able to force the USSR to recognize that war and aggression were unprofitable, when it withdrew into isolation, floundering on internal problems, it lost credibility with the outside world and no strategy could succeed. The situation was made even worse by a steady decline of US military power.

THE DECLINE OF AMERICAN MILITARY POWER

Throughout the period of détente, the strategic position of the United States worsened while the Soviet position improved. Precise figures for military spending in the USSR are not known: official figures are too low to be credible. Estimates made in the West vary, but they all detect a regular rise in capability during the two decades in question: the debate hinges on the growth rate of expenditure, not on growth itself. The CIA gave 4-5% as a yearly average over twenty years; it estimated the share of this expenditure of the Soviet Union's GNP to have remained almost level between 11 and 13%. Figures in American military spending, on the other hand, showed a steady decrease. The defense budget went from 11% of GNP in 1967-68 to less than 7% in 1972-73. This development, in Nixon's opinion, was the result of the CIA underestimating Soviet strategic spending in the 1960s and early 1970s, thus affecting American armament programs. According to him, from 1973 to the end of the decade, the USSR attributed to the strategic sector three times as many resources as the United States. A study published in *Foreign Affairs* (1983, Number 3) indicates that American military spending fell from $130 billion to 96 billion between 1968 and 1977, while in the Soviet Union it rose from $101 to 130 billion, prices remaining constant. The Stockholm Institute for Peace Research (*SIPRI Yearbook, 1980*, pp. 19 and 29) advanced different figures, but comparable. From research data established for a Rand Corporation report, the CIA showed a steeper rise in Soviet expenditure after the SALT agreement of 1972.

Thus détente did influence the trend affecting the years previous to SALT-1, in the late 1960s: increase of military spending on the Soviet side, decrease on the American side. SALT-1 was not followed by a slowing down of the Soviet effort, nor of its growth rate. The Americans had hoped that the talks with Moscow would lead to a balance in strategic weapons. About half-way through the 1970s, they realized that they were wrong: the Soviets went on strengthening their capability while, on the American side part, they were applying the brakes. From then on, they would keep a watchful eye on the situation.

Why did the Soviet leaders behave in such a way, signing the SALT-1 agreement while continuing their strategic build-up? Various answers come to mind and there in no consensus in the United States on this point. Two elements emerge to answer this question. If the Soviets were keen to negotiate the agreement, i.e., institute a control on the arms race, it was probably not in order to reduce their capability but to allow them to develop their defense programs more leisurely, free from the pressure of American advances. If they did not go into lower gear, it was due to the fact that military power, to their mind, was obviously a key element of dialogue with the United States. Détente was based on a balance of forces. It occurred in an environment of competition between the two systems and there was no question of it leading to a weakening of the USSR; the Soviets also were convinced that the United States had been brought to the negotiating table by their rival's power. Therefore reinforcing the Soviet military machine would incite the Americans to continue the dialogue. There could be no relaxation in this respect, since Soviet power did not lie in the economy nor the ideology. In fact, concerning the economy, the Soviet Union had given up trying to emulate its rival. Power had to be political and military. In strategic armaments, parity had been won and the circumstances (i.e., the SALT agreement and slowing down of the American defense effort) made it possible to forge ahead. Thus the Soviet leaders decided to concentrate all their energies in this sector to develop their power, since they believed that it was the only way to prevent the United States banning them again from the international community and thwarting their interests.

The USSR's approach seems to have had no connection either with the course taken by détente or the Americans' behavior. It seemed to the leaders that only strength could ensure the success of cooperation with the West, which meant that every effort had to be made to develop their war machine. The relative decline of the American strategic power meant an advance for the other superpower, as well as a cause for satisfaction when reality proved disappointing. Dialogue did not produce everything that had been hoped for. Yet in spite of a few setbacks, given the opponent's weaker position, it might still be useful not to break off relations. For the United States, whatever caused the situation to deteriorate, it was a bitter disappointment.

TIME FOR A REAPPRAISAL

By 1973-1974 things had gone seriously wrong; half-way through the decade the talks broke down irretrievably.

In the United States, the October war was the first episode in the downward spiral: the part played by the USSR in the conflict stirred old feelings of distrust in public opinion. The Jackson Amendment affair seriously affected the situation and made President Nixon practically powerless, while his strategy plummeted to the ground. In the matter of nuclear weapons, the United States realized that arms control was anything but easy to enforce. It did not take long for them to find out that the USSR were steadily building up it military capability, which the Americans found intolerable. But to top it all, the USSR started making trouble in Angola and countless disappointments met every American effort to improve relations. Henry Kissinger, under President Ford, could not redress the situation. Not until Jimmy Carter took over did the Americans base their foreign policy no longer on "great powers" relations, as Richard Nixon had done, but on solving global problems like human rights or nuclear non-proliferation, and on establishing some sort of world order, in which the USSR could, if it wished, participate, but under conditions chosen by others, without consultation between the superpowers, with the only alternative being isolation—it was essentially back to square one. After hoping to reach a state of peaceful coexistence with the USSR, the US had to admit failure. Yet the responsibility was partly on its side.

In the USSR, as in the United States, the idea of détente having failed took root in 1973 and grew during the next three years. The Middle East was for Moscow, too, the first hurdle on which détente stumbled: between the October war (1973) and 1975, it understood that dialogue with the United States did not lead to shared responsibilities, but to a serious weakening of its positions in a region which it had long considered as vital, while the United States improved theirs. The Jackson affair in 1973-1974 demonstrated to the Soviet leaders that détente had not fundamentally altered the conception of the United States vis-à-vis them and their actions, as had been expected, consequently relations remained basically unchanged; they also realized that the American executive was not capable of enforcing this policy.

Half way through the 1970s, the USSR had another reason for unease: relations recently established by certain East European countries with the West resulted in an impasse. These initiatives were intended to solve political and economic difficulties, especially in Poland. After Gomulka fell from power late in 1970, his successor, E. Gierek, who was western-oriented and a pragmatist, looked for a new model of development. Unlike his predecessor for whom economic self-sufficiency was a basic principle, he decided to rely on the West to raise the standard of living, encourage production through technological transfer and western capital, and achieve a better balance. The economic results that he achieved to start with made it possible to introduce a certain liberalization in politics. In the early 1970s, Poland projected the attractive image of a country willing and able to change: it had become a bridge between Eastern and Western Europe. Moscow was, in the beginning, highly satisfied with this development which coincided with the privileged relations it was enjoying with the United States and raised the communist bloc's reputation abroad. Dialogue with Washington had everything to gain from the situation which would also improve the climate in Europe, thereby giving a better chance of success to the talks on European security that started in 1973. On the spot, it became easier to attract foreign investments which were needed for the policy adopted by Gierek. Moscow was all the more inclined to accept this venture since it had reduced the risks of exposure to the capitalist world by tightening relations inside the socialist camp. At the beginning of the decade, exchanges between the various parts of the bloc had been reorganized to make them more dependent on one another.

Success was short-lived, however. "Towards the middle 1970s, the consensus that Gierek tried to establish met with a dual crisis, a political one late in 1975, compounded by an economic one in 1976." In 1975, the Constitutional Reform imposed on Poland and her allies by the USSR raised an outcry. The intelligentsia rejected the articles of the new Constitution which severely limited internal and external independence for the Polish state. Moscow was much concerned by the mood of rebellion. Each time the socialist camp was divided, it became apparent, as Carrère d'Encausse put it in her book *Le Grand Frère*, that the "rebels" always showed a strong "desire to join the international community by denying the existence of a specific socialist community and privileged bonds between its members." The Polish intelligentsia's reaction was proof of the reappearance of this phenomenon. The USSR was appalled; it became aware that, in spite of the measures taken, exchanges with the West introduced a climate of permissiveness and had a serious social impact. Untold consequences might affect the internal balance of the satellite countries and destroy the cohesion of its Empire. The only remedy was to reverse the policy of contacts with the West for the entire bloc. The events of 1976 only confirmed the wisdom of this decision. Poland was engulfed into another crisis, this time economic—to begin with at least—but it soon assumed considerable proportions. The intelligentsia unanimously sided with the workers and the Church also took up their cause. The whole political structure was shaken: Gierek's recipe had failed. The results were disastrous from a political as well as an economic point of view. During the following months, in Romania workers' strikes and human rights protests erupted. This "rebellious ally" of Moscow, fiercely jealous of its independence, was a special case in Eastern Europe. If unrest spread, external pressures would be much stronger than elsewhere in the communist camp. The balance would be disrupted and disastrous consequences would follow from the Soviet angle.

In the middle of the decade, Moscow's leaders had drawn their conclusions: détente, as it had been outlined in 1972-73, was leading nowhere. They had to change direction. Even if they wished to carry on, it was no longer possible since their counterpart had vanished. The American executive power was in a state of collapse after failing to enforce its policy.

Basing themselves on this observation, the Soviets looked for a way out which would introduce the post-détente period under manageable conditions. The Portuguese withdrawal from the African colonies gave them an opportunity to display their power and increase it, to compensate for their loss of influence in the Middle East, to prove to the men who had blamed them earlier for their internal regulations that they were in a position to make their mark in distant parts of the world—this was most important. They had a free hand in the enterprise, as the United States did not react.

Détente meant a combination of talks and competition. The moment the former proved a failure, balance between the two was broken and competition gained the upper-hand. The United States, at this point, made it easy for the USSR: as American power subsided, a situation was created which was to the USSR's advantage. There had been a hope that the Soviets' international behavior would become less aggressive if they were caught in a web of agreements which they would be loath to put at risk. At the time of the Angola affair, the Americans were surprised to see that the latter did not weigh the advantages to be derived from cooperation against a risky venture in foreign policy. In reality, events did not turn out to enable them to verify the soundness of this reasoning. Cooperation might have exerted a moderating influence *if* dialogue had produced results. Since the Soviet leaders did not obtain what was essential to them— recognition of their status as full members of the international community on a par with the greatest world power—anything else (economic, scientific, technical and cultural cooperation) no longer counted. In these fields a start had been made: they fully believed that the flow of information and goods would not be easy to inter-rupt for some time and they would still be able to benefit from it in the near future. In any case, if the Americans drew their conclusions and backed down—the USSR would be able to find alternative sources. In the strategic sector, cooperation had progressed to such an extent that it would take a long time to reverse it; by then the Soviets would have forged ahead.

Thus, in the mid-1970s, while the Soviet leaders saw that dialogue with Washington had not given them complete satisfaction and that it was in their interest to change their approach to the West, they retained some hope of a reversal of the situation. They consid-ered their failure at preserving a climate of cooperation as a serious setback. Yet they believed that, due to the United States' loss of influence, they could overcome this disappointment through a more advantageous power position. In the strategic area they were gaining fast. In Africa they demonstrated that success in international affairs did not require sharing responsibility with the United States. Relations with the West had also made possible a long-term project of theirs, the Conference on European Security. On August 1, 1975, the final meeting ended with a bang and the assembled leaders signed a law endorsing the status quo in Europe. This put a seal on the division of Europe and implicitly endorsed Soviet influence in Eastern Europe. All in all, the decade had been satisfactory, with gains fairly balancing failures.

10

WHAT WAS LEFT OF DÉTENTE?

Both Nixon's and Brezhnev's ambition was to stabilize mutual relations and organize foreign affairs in such a way as to prevent local conflicts from encroaching on their dialogue. After ten years, no one could deny that relations between the superpowers were more strained than they had been for a long time. Intergovernmental talks had broken down, the strategic situation was ominous, the international balance of forces, after being subjected to severe crises, was precarious—in short, the Soviet leaders were becoming unpredictable.

Brezhnev and Nixon had meant to hold meetings on a regular basis to be able to compare each other's points of view and eventually agree on what should be done. These good intentions did not last because of the difficulties encountered by each country and Nixon's departure. Since the Vladivostok meeting in November 1974, Carter and Brezhnev met once only, in Vienna in June 1979. President Reagan never met his Soviet opposite number. The days of frequent meetings between Kissinger and Dobrynin seemed gone forever. Talks between the Secretary of State and the Soviet Foreign Minister had become erratic. The notion of concerted action was a thing of the past, and after the Soviet invasion of Afghanistan, communication broke down altogether.

Dialogue wasn't only about meetings and discussions. It also meant privileged relations, which were priceless to the USSR. The position the latter had enjoyed as a privileged partner of the greatest world power was a thing of the past. While the Nixon-Kissinger team had centered world affairs on full cooperation between the two countries, on a basis of equality, the Carter administration's world view brought it down to the level of one among many other aims. There was no longer room for initiative or joint exercise of power with the United States. The Nixon government had stressed the importance of relations between the great powers (USA, Soviet Union, China); the Carter one focused its attention primarily on relations with the United States' allies and the Third World, together with global problems such as human rights and nuclear non-proliferation. These efforts met with varying success but indicated a wish to be guided by more idealistic principles, in contrast with the realistic approach of Nixon and Kissinger. The one saw Third World conflicts as manifestations of Soviet hostility towards the West, while the other considered them as arising from local circumstances. Under Carter's presidency no thought was given to sharing responsibilities, as had been the case under Nixon.

Under Reagan, the Soviet Union was back in the center of world politics, but the situation was radically different from what it had been ten years earlier. The conclusion that Carter's successor came to, after summing up the lessons of the 1970s, was that the USSR had to be considered as a threat (mainly from the military point of view) because it sought to expand its empire. He did not view relations with Moscow from the angle of confrontation only, but judged it advisable to re-define détente: the United States had to reaffirm its authority in world affairs, be more demanding with the USSR, and show determination in those dealings. What bode ill for Moscow was that, as Carter had done, he put relations into a moral perspective. Thus he rejected one of the main claims made by the Soviets: to be treated on a par with any other state, to bring the West to renounce moral judgments on their internal affairs. Nixon had attempted to see relations with Moscow in this impartial light. His successors, on the contrary, thought the United States had to be careful in dealing with a country whose philosophy was so different from theirs.

The USSR, instead of remaining a privileged partner of the United States as it had been in the early 1970s, looked now like the Public Enemy Number One, while China has lost all credibility as a menace to the Americans. The Soviets felt bitter about this development, but were partly responsible for it. Their military build-up and their activities in the Third World deeply disturbed American public opinion and played havoc in international relations.

SALT-1 did not achieve arms control. It is true that the negotiations which had started in 1969 continued in spite of many obstacles. On June 18, 1979, in Vienna, Jimmy Carter and Leonid Brezhnev signed the SALT-2 treaty—the agreement establishing a similar ceiling for both parties was operational until December 31, 1985—and decided jointly to continue negotiations towards SALT-3. In 1969, a process of uninterrupted discussions started which was to last for fourteen years. These SALT talks, which became "START" talks when President Reagan insisted on reducing armaments rather than limiting them only, were suspended on December 8, 1983, by the Soviets as a protest against the implementation of the twin decision made by NATO, in December 1979, concerning ICBMs. All was not lost, however. One year later, on January 8, 1985, the US Secretary of State, George Shultz, and his Soviet counterpart, Andrei Gromyko, decided to resume talks in Geneva, in March, under a different heading this time, since they would deal not only with strategic weapons, but also ICBMs and the so-called "Star Wars" system.

The outcome of the discussions was not up to the expectations that had been raised. The controversial SALT-2 treaty was never ratified by the American Senate, because it was deemed unsatisfactory as a means of armament control and not compatible with the demands of American security. The Soviet invasion of Afghanistan dealt another blow to the ratification process and President Carter asked the Senate to suspend the debate. Some time later, President Reagan put an end to all proceedings. The two treaties on limitation of underground testing of nuclear weapons dated July 3, 1974 and May 28, 1976, were not ratified by Congress either. In all three cases, there was tacit agreement between the two parties to respect the clauses. Nevertheless it could be called a failure, not only because the American government later suspected the Soviet leaders of acting in breach of the agreements, but also because competition between them went on as previously. The USSR proceeded with massive military build-up. After a while the pace slowed down: the CIA, in November 1983, released figures that were lower than previous estimates: the yearly growth of Soviet military expenditure, which had been on average from 4 to 5% between 1966 and 1976, went down to about 2% since then. Yet, even if these figures were accurate and the USSR had slowed down the rate of increase in military spending, it remained at a very high level, much higher than was needed for defensive purposes only. Moreover this build up incited the United States, after the period of moderation mentioned above, to reverse its policy: to regain the edge over the USSR, it increased its military budget again and reactivated programs that had been suspended or abandoned in the 1970s.

The Soviet increase in both offensive and defensive capability had a negative effect on strategic stability. After 1972, while remaining within the limits set by SALT-1, a new generation of ballistic missiles was deployed (ICBMs SS-17, SS-19 and SS-18, the SLBMs SS-NX-17 and SS-N-18), which made the situation highly unstable: the SS-19 carried three times and the SS-18 seven times further than the Minuteman-3. The new Soviet offensive weapons, known to be highly accurate, could reach American ICBM silos with increased probability, thereby depriving the US of its response. The rules of deterrence no longer applied. The United States felt the need to protect its silos.

In the field of anti-ballistic missile defense (BMD), the USSR took such giant strides that an increasing number of Western analysts wondered whether it had signed the 1972 ABM treaty because it wished to base strategic stability on reciprocal vulnerability or because it aimed at catching up with the United States.

Much to the dismay of European countries, there followed a resumption of the defensive arms race which had been under control for ten years. This was made possible by the advances occurring since 1972, any further developments in this direction seeming at this time too costly and unrealistic. In March 1983, President Reagan gave the go-ahead for a new push in the development of BMD systems, asking "the scientific community which gave us nuclear weapons […] to provide us with the means to render these weapons powerless and make them obsolescent." The Soviets reacted strongly to the American plans, though they were directly related to the advances made by the USSR.

Détente opened the way for a strengthening of the Soviet military power as well as increased Soviet involvement on the inter-national scene, which the Americans found intolerable. These two factors made the balance of forces at the time give the advantage to the Soviet Union. In the second half of the 1970s, Moscow carried out a policy of aggression in Third World countries which deeply disturbed both the US and international relations. In Africa, its actions were highly successful in three directions: in the south (the USSR became involved in Angola and also Mozambique with which a treaty of friendship and cooperation was signed on March 31, 1977), the Horn of Africa (its support of Ethiopia in 1977-78 was huge and a treaty was signed in November 1978), and the African coast. Bases strung down the coast allowed the USSR naval facilities and permit-ted deployment of its navy, which could become a threat to the West as the Soviet navy had grown into a considerable world power; they also made it possible to keep a watch on sea highways and to make their presence felt in countries further inland: without access to the sea, most of their economies could not survive. These developments illustrated the new direction taken by Soviet foreign policy: not content with the control of satellite countries, the leaders wanted to be able to intervene in the Third World and have a say in the settle-ment of conflicts. The Americans were dismayed to find out that the

USSR was in a position to have a global policy (but in the late 1970s, they refused to compete in distant ventures).

The Soviets took full advantage of a weaker American executive and lack of purpose: it was tempting to seize the initiative in the face of American inertia. Yet this factor does not fully account for the Soviet foreign policy followed at the time. It partly answered a wish to compensate for loss of influence in the Middle East and above all it arose from a sense of competition with China which had become deeply involved in African affairs. While in the 1950s and 1960s, Soviet aid to the continent stood much higher than the Chinese aid, after 1970 the situation was the opposite. Between 1970 and 1976, China became the main communist partner of Africa. This development made Moscow nervous, especially since it was not confined to one part of the world.

After 1975, China became involved in many areas of the world. From 1977-78, it launched a many-sided diplomatic offensive and established economic relations with Western industrial countries. It put out feelers to India (when the Janata party was in power between 1977 and 1980) when privileged Soviet-Indian relations were a pillar of Soviet Asian policy. China signed a peace treaty with Japan, on August 12, 1978, which regularized their relations (which the USSR had failed to do). In January 1979, diplomatic relations were established with the United States, putting an official seal to the rapprochement started in 1971. These initiatives were seen by the USSR as a threat since there was a risk of the latter becoming isolated. It was imperative not to give a free hand to Beijing; Soviet positions were consolidated in Asia to contain China. Within a few months, relations with Vietnam became closer (up to this time the two communist powers' influence had been evenly matched) and it joined the socialist camp: Hanoi was integrated into COMECON on June 29, 1978, and on November 3 of that year signed a treaty of friendship and cooperation with Moscow. The USSR started to press for a Union of Indo-Chinese countries under the aegis of Vietnam (in January 1979, the Vietnamese army launched an offensive against Cambodia which ended with the Khmer Rouge having to bow out and a handful of men taking over power with Hanoi's backing)— such a Union lying immediately to the south of China gave the Soviet Union a powerful advantage.

The invasion of Afghanistan in December 1979, a few months later, reinforced Soviet positions to the northeast of the Chinese rival. This was the start of a serious international crisis when relations with the West slumped. Since the end of the war, it was the first instance of the USSR embarking on military intervention in a country lying outside its sphere of influence (i.e., Eastern Europe). In the Third World, it had acted through an ally (Cubans in Angola and Ethiopia, Vietnamese in Cambodia). In this case, a sovereign country was invaded and there was no likelihood of Soviet troops ever being withdrawn. What brought about this new venture? Several explanations come to mind: China was given proof positive that the USSR had no intention of letting her have a free hand in Asia, Soviet capacity to intervene wherever was opportune was demonstrated, the collapse of a friendly regime recently established on its border was avoided. The Soviet leaders refused to allow the country to return to the old regime, which would set a precedent for other nations in the empire. Whatever might be the reasons for an intervention, it was clear that the reaction of the US did not enter the mind of the Soviet authorities. The Carter government was indignant and Soviet-American relations reached an all time low.

International tension on the whole remained high. After 1980, events in Poland gave the situation a more acute turn. From the Western point of view, the emergence of a strong autonomous trade union in Poland might have been a symbol of better East-West relations. The announcement of martial law on December 13, 1981, followed by Solidarity being banned a few months later, demonstrated clearly the Soviet leaders' rejection of a more relaxed atmosphere eventually leading to democratization inside the bloc, and therefore of a wish to put relations with the West high on their agenda. This attitude was to be expected: in a political system in which the leaders drew their legitimacy from identifying with society, the fact that a free trade union existed undermined the regime's foundations. But it was a useful reminder to the West that the Soviets would not allow the chance of improving East-West relations to weaken the ideological basis of socialism.

Tensions increased with the Euromissile crisis. The USSR broke negotiations on military matters when the Americans, in response to the threat posed by the Soviet SS-20, late in 1983, started to deploy their new Cruise missiles in Europe in accordance with a decision approved by NATO in 1979. Things had reached an impasse.

Soviet behavior in international affairs altered significantly after the failure of détente. The same happened in domestic affairs. The Soviet leaders stiffened up and withdrew from outside contact; they no longer sought acceptance by the West. On September 1, 1983, the destruction of a civilian aircraft, the South Korean Boeing which, by mistake, had entered Soviet air space, sadly proved the point. Harassment of dissidents, not so brazen for a while, was resumed with a vengeance: in January 1980, Sakharov, exiled to Gorki, lived in complete isolation; the movements in defense of human rights which had sprung up following the Helsinki agreements were systematically repressed. The Kremlin leaders were clearly signaling to the West that they were willing to respect agreements only if these suited them.

Nixon and Brezhnev had hoped that economic, commercial, scientific and technical cooperation would have a stabilizing influence. It appears that they were wrong. Nixon had also hoped that the new climate would make it possible to exert pressure on the Soviets to direct them this way or that and that it could be used as a reward when the USSR acted in accordance with American interests. This also proved to be an illusion. Under the impulse given at the start of the decade, collaboration took off and, although with mixed results and some hiccoughs, it advanced steadily in the face of worsening political relations. Scientific and technical cooperation was suspended briefly following the Angolan crisis but went ahead later. The agreements signed between 1972 and 1974 were renewed five years later, as planned. The Afghanistan intervention, the establishment of martial law in Poland and the downing of the South Korean airplane caused more prolonged interruptions. Cooperation almost came to a standstill following these events: it went down by 80% between 1979 and 1983. Yet a number of agreements were renewed in 1982-83 (agriculture, health, peaceful use of nuclear energy, environment and construction); four of them were not extended (the May 24, 1972, basic agreement—those on energy, space exploration and peaceful use of the cosmos, on transport). Towards the end of 1984, there was a tendency to reopen contacts and negotiations so as to reach agreements on current problems.

The same phenomenon occurred in trade, even more markedly, as cooperation grew throughout the 1970s. By 1976, it had increased four-fold compared to 1972 and by 1978, ten-fold compared with 1971. A record was reached in 1979 with 2.8 billion rubles. From 1966 to 1970 the total amounted to 0.6 billion rubles; from 1971 to 1975: 4.2 billion and for the four following years, 8.4 billion. The increase was spectacular, even though the figures must be revised, since they are at current prices. From the impulse they received early in the 1970s, exchanges acquired their own dynamism. In other words, in spite of their aggressive foreign policy, the Soviet leaders, to a certain extent, continued to benefit from the incentive of trade. In this respect, events in Afghanistan and Poland had an impact on the situation: exchanges in 1980 dropped by half over the previous year and remained below the original level in later years. The United States' share of Soviet imports of cereals was reduced to 20% in 1980 and 1981 compared to an average of 60% between 1972 and 1980. Yet the trend remained and political considerations were not sufficient to thwart trade relations, since other factors came in to play, such as European and Japanese competition (Argentinean in the case of cereals) and pressure from American farmers, regardless of the political context.

Deals concerning cereals are the best example of this phenomenon. Each time a crisis erupted, the United States undertook sanctions in this field but those were soon lifted, in complete disregard of political developments, because it did not serve US interests to keep them in force. After the Afghanistan invasion, on January 4, 1980, President Carter announced that American deliveries would be reduced to a minimum (the threshold of 8 million tons laid down in the 1975 agreement became operative, while the Soviet Union had ordered 25 million). His successor, President Ronald Reagan, lifted these restrictions one year later, on April 25, 1981. (This does not mean they had no impact—the Soviets were faced with a shortage of cereals and the United States had showed their mettle in the face of harmful consequences for their economy.)

In December 1981, following the imposition of martial law in Poland, President Reagan decided to postpone negotiations for another long-term agreement. This decision was obviously not in the interest of the United States: the reasons which, in 1975, had made it decide to introduce regulations for transactions were still valid. Six months later, on July 30, 1982, Reagan extended the 1975 agreement by a year (which was to expire on September 30); and on October 15, he undertook to deliver up to 23 million tons in cereals to the USSR, much in excess of what had been settled in the 1975 convention. On April 22, 1983, he proved even more flexible when he offered to open negotiations for another long-term agreement with Moscow. This was duly signed on July 28, 1983, to be valid for five years: a minimum of 9 to 12 million tons would be delivered yearly. One year later, on September 11, 1984, the American president raised the ceiling—from 12 it went to 22 million tons. These deals were unprecedented in the history of relations between the two countries. They created a lasting bond between them which had first been established at the start of détente, early in the 1970s. In the American trade policy, they occupied a special position; it was no longer hoped that they would play a part in making Soviet internal policy more flexible and encourage a more moderate manner in international affairs, but they embodied a realization that the interests of the two countries did sometimes coincide.

Cooperation in commerce and science did not expand as much as it would have if political relations had been more stable, remaining far below the level it could have reached. Yet early in the 1980s, in spite of difficulties, trade remained higher than it had been in pre-détente days. Moscow constantly pleaded for an increase, but appreciated whatever benefit détente had brought.

Though Moscow was aware of its failure to achieve stable relations with Washington and wished it had been otherwise, it had gained considerable advantages in the post-détente period. The Americans were deeply disappointed at the extent of their failure. This does not mean that they gained nothing from the policy chosen for the 1970s, apart from a few cereal deals. Détente significantly influenced East-West relations and even if the United States did not directly benefit from the new climate, it was an achievement. Since the early 1970s, the situation of the USSR on the world stage had greatly altered, not only because the rapprochement with the US increased its power, but also because its relations with the outside world were different. It was no longer isolated.

However much the Kremlin might have wished to keep contacts to a minimum and in spite of repression, Soviet society was more open than it had been. It was more accessible to external influences; emigration, still on a modest scale, became a factor on the political scene; relations with the West were more extensive; Western trends in lifestyle were gaining ground (significantly the young developed a strong liking for modern music and jeans); watch committees concerned with the implementation of the convention on human rights of the Helsinki treaty had been silenced, but they had not disappeared completely; books published in the West, written by Westerners or Soviet émigrés, circulated in large numbers in the USSR; Western programs in the Russian language gained large audiences during the 1970s. Eastern Europe moved nearer to Western European countries. The trend towards a more balanced economic development, more consumer-oriented, became more marked in the USSR as well as in Eastern Europe.

Meanwhile, the USSR had been forced to admit its economic difficulties, in particular its chronic inability to remedy food shortages. While pre-1917 Russia had a surplus of cereals, the USSR in the 1970s could not even feed its citizens. The first socialist country, to make up for crop shortfalls and ensure a satisfactory level of food supply for its population, was reduced to purchasing several million tons of cereals every year from the top capitalist country, which enjoyed large surpluses of agricultural produce. This was a situation which could only affect adversely the USSR's public image, especially in Third World countries which were particularly concerned with problems of food supplies.

A positive element in the world situation of the 1970s was the fact that a balance between the superpowers had been achieved, willy-nilly. The arms race was still on and stability left much to be desired, but local crises erupting all over the globe—in the Middle East as in Central America, in Asia or Africa—did not result either in direct confrontation between the United States and the Soviet Union or in a nuclear conflict, something which in the atomic era was not to be despised.

Was failure unavoidable? The moment the American executive power collapsed, no doubt the answer was "yes." History shows that the Soviet leaders found it difficult not to take advantage of any opportunity to build up their security forces, first and foremost, and also their prestige and power. The fact that the Soviet Union had a dynamic notion of détente, that this was just a means to enhance its position vis-à-vis its rival and work for the advancement of socialism, does not mean that failure was inevitable. It was up to the Americans to meet the challenge, to resist Soviet pressures and to demonstrate the vitality of their social and political system.

Secondly, when China's involvement in other countries' affairs threatened to isolate the USSR or even to assert its presence excessively, the plan was doomed to failure. It was not because the Soviet leaders accused the Americans of having a part in it, but they were incited to take violent action to curb the initiative of their brother-adversary, at the cost of any other consideration. The force of their response was bound to affect relations with Washington.

If these two issues had been out of the way, the chances of the project succeeding become clearer. The Americans did not wish to share the world with the Soviets, nor to allow them to intervene in areas where they could act on their own (in the Middle East, for example). In this sense, there was no likelihood of the Soviet Union having its way. True in the strategic field, though the goal of arms control was difficult enough to reach because of the incredibly complex problems to solve, it was even more so from the political point of view. The USSR was convinced that power was the basis of dialogue and armaments was an area where the most rapid progress could be made.

Economic and scientific cooperation did continue to a certain extent and would have probably developed further, if the political climate had been favorable and if cooperation had been freed from political implications.

As regards dialogue itself, meaning a desire for communication, it was all-important for both parties owing to its impact on the balance of forces in the world. Moscow had everything to gain from it, considering the prestige attached to it, and there are chances that it might have lasted longer than it did. Nixon and Brezhnev tried very hard. In the light of experience, they tried too hard. They might have obtained better results if they had been content with limited objectives in political, economic and scientific partnership, and if dialogue had not been made conditional on the USSR accepting Western rules of conduct.

The complexity of decision-making in the United States, the power exercised by interest groups, the influence of public opinion over the body politic, all affected the course taken by the American government. These elements were underestimated by Nixon and should not have been overlooked in such a sensitive and controversial area as relations with the Soviet Union.

These remarks lead to a second question: will the USSR and the United States ever come to an understanding? History shows that straight is the gate and possibilities for agreement few. But superpowers have to live together in the nuclear era. The stakes are too high to accept failure and some dialogue has to be established. The policy carried out by President Reagan during his first mandate made matters worse. The Soviet leaders were angered by his lack of comprehension, but maybe in the long-term his insistence on a powerful American nation was not entirely negative. A new balance may be established and better relations ensue. However, détente will never be more than a dream, even if a revival of the policy launched by Richard Nixon and Leonid Brezhnev were to appear possible at times.

SELECTIVE BIBLIOGRAPHY

THE USSR OF THE EARLY 1970S AND ITS FOREIGN POLICY

G. Arbatov. *Lutte idéologique et relations internationales*. Moscow, 1974.

L.I. Brezhnev. *Peace, Détente, Cooperation*. New York, 1981.

H. Carrère d'Encause. *La politique Soviétique au Moyen-Orient — 1955-1975*. Paris, 1976.

———. *Le pouvoir confisqué*. Paris, 1980.

———. *Le Grand Frère*. Paris, 1983.

Congressional Research Service of the Library of Congress. *Soviet Diplomacy and Negotiating Behavior: Emerging New Context for US Diplomacy*, vol. 1. Washington, 1979.

A. Fontaine. *Historie de la guerre Froide*, tome II: 1950-1971. Paris, 1976.

———. *Un seul lit pour deux rêves*. Paris, 1981.

R. Fritsch-Bournazel. *L'Union Soviétique et les Allemagnes*. Paris, 1979.

A. Gromyko. *La politique extérieure: leçons et réalités — les années 60 et 70*. Moscow, 1978.

K. Jowitt. *Images of Détente and the Soviet Political Order*. Berkeley, 1977.

R.E. Kanet. *Soviet Foreign Policy and East-West Relations*. New York, 1982.

W. Laqueur. *La vraie guerre du Kippour*. Paris, 1974.

N.I. Lebedev. *A New Stage in International Relations*. Oxford/New York, 1978 (ed. soviétique 1976).

J. Levesque. *L'URSS et sa politique internationale de 1917 à nos jours.* Paris, 1980.

_____. *Le Conflit sino-soviétique.* Paris, 1973.

A. Sakharov. *Progress, Coexistence and Intellectual Freedom.* New York, 1968.

_____. *Mon pays et le monde.* Paris, 1975.

A. Soljenitsyne. *Discours Américains.* Paris, 1975.

M. Tatu. *Le triangle Washington-Moscou-Pékin et les deux Europe(s).* Paris, 1972.

P. Wajsman. *L'illusion de la détente.* Paris, 1977.

W. Welch. *American Images of Soviet Foreign Policy.* New Haven, 1970.

THE UNITED STATES AND ITS FOREIGN POLICY

C. Bell. *The Diplomacy of Détente: The Kissinger era.* New York, 1977.

Congressional Research Service. *US Foreign Policy for the 1970's. An analysis of the president's 1973 Foreign Policy Report and Congressional Action.* Washington, 1973.

S.J. Erwin. *The Whole Truth: The Watergate Conspiracy.* New York, 1980.

A. Grosser. *Les Occidentaux — les pays d'Europe et les Etats-Unis depuis la guerre.* Paris, 1978.

S. Hoffman. *Le dilemme américain — suprématie ou ordre mondiale.* Paris, 1982.

M. Jobert. *L'autre regard.* Paris, 1976.

P.M. Kattenburg. *The Vietnam Trauma in American Foreign Policy, 1945-1975.* New Brunswick. 1980.

H. Kissinger. *A La Maison Blanche, 1968-1973* (in the text as M.B.). 2 volumes. Paris, 1979.

____. *Les Années Orageuses* (in the text as A.O.). Paris, 1982.

____. *Nuclear Weapons and Foreign Policy*, New York, 1957.

A. Kaspi. *Le Watergate*. Bruxelles, 1983.

M. Mansfield, US Senate. *European Reactions to the Soviet-United States Détente*. Report to the Committee on Foreign Relations. Washington, 1973.

R. Nixon. *Mémories*. Montréal, 1978.

____. *La Vraie Guerre*. Paris, 1980.

D.S. Papp. *Vietnam — The View from Moscow, Peking, Washington*. Caroline du Nord, 1981.

F. Snepp. *Sauve qui peut*. Paris, 1977.

THE DÉTENTE AND SOVIET-AMERICAN RELATIONS

D. Caldwell. *American-Soviet Relations form 1947 to the Nixon-Kissinger Grand Design*. London, 1981.

J.L. Gaddis. *Russia, the Soviet Union and the U.S.: An Interpretative History*. New York, 1978.

Ch. et T.T. Gati. *The Debate over Détente*. New York, 1977.

House of Representatives, Committee on Foreign Affairs. *Détente*, Hearings. Washington, 1974.

G.F. Kennan. *Le Mirage Nucléaire. Les relations américano-soviétique à l'âge de l'atome*. Paris, 1983.

R. Pipes. *US-Soviet Relations in the era of Détente*. Colorado, 1981.

Les Rapports soviéto-américains — bilan et perspectives. Moscow, 1975.

N.V. Sivachev and N.N. Yakovlev. *Russia and the United States: US-Soviet Relations from the Soviet Point of View*. Chicago, 1979.

A. Ulam. *Dangerous Relations — The Soviet Union in World Politics, 1970-1982*. New York, 1983.

SALT I AND DEFENSE QUESTIONS

A.J. Alexander, A.S. Becker, W.E. Hoehn, Jr. *The Significance of Divergent US-USSR Military Expenditures*. Rand Corporation, 1979.

A.S. Becker. *The Burden of Soviet Defense: A Political-Economic Essay*. Rand Corporation, 1981.

D. Brennan, ed. *Arms Control, Disarmament and National Security*. New York, 1961.

L.T. Caldwell. *Soviet Attitudes to SALT*. Adelphi Papers no. 75, 1971.

C.I.A. National Foreign Assessment Center. *Estimated Soviet Defense Spending: Trends and Prospects*. 1978.

J. Newhouse. *Cold Dawn: The Story of SALT*. New York, 1974.

C.M. Roberts. *The Nuclear Years. The Arms Race and Arms Control, 1945-1970*. New York, 1970.

G.C. Smith. *Doubletalk: The Story of the First Strategic Arms Limitation Talks*. New York, 1980.

COMMERCE AND ECONOMIC RELATIONS

M.I. Goldman. *Détente and Dollars — Doing Business with the Soviets*. New York, 1975.

J.P. Hardt and G.D. Holliday. *US-Soviet Commercial Relations: The Interplay of Economics, Technology Transfer and Diplomacy*. House of Representatives: Washington, 1973.

G.D. Holliday. *Technology Transfer to the USSR, 1928-1937 and 1966-1977: The Role of Western Technology in Soviet Economic Development.* Colorado, 1979.

Joint Economic Committee, US Congress. *Observations on East-West Economic Relations: USSR and Poland.* Washington, 1973.

M. Lavigne. *Les relations économiques Est-Ouest.* Paris, 1979.

R. Morton, US Department of Commerce. *The US role in East-West Trade — Problems and Prospects.* Washington, 1975.

P.G. Peterson, US Department of Commerce. *US-Soviet Commercial Relations in a New Era.* Washington, 1972.

S. Pisar. *Les armes de la paix. L'ouverture économique vers l'Est.* Paris, 1970.

_____. *Transactions entre l'Est et l'Ouest — Le cadre commercial et juridique.* Paris, 1972.

G. Sokoloff. *L'économie de la détente: l'URSS et le capital occidental.* Paris. 1983.

US Senate, Committee on Government Operations. *Russian Grain Transactions*, Hearings. Washington, 1973.

SCIENTIFIC, TECHNOLOGICAL AND CULTURAL COOPERATION

Congressional Research Service. *Technology Transfer and Scientific Cooperation between the United States and the Soviet Union: A Review.* Washington, 1977.

House of Representatives, Committee on Science and Technology. *Review of US-USSR Cooperative Agreements on Science and Technology.* Special oversight report no. 6. Washington, 1976.

House of Representatives, Committee on Science and Technology. *Key Issues in US-USSR Scientific Exchanges and Technology Transfers.* Washington, 1979.